STUDIES IN THE GERMANIC LANGUAGES AND LITERATURES

Number 5

EDITORIAL COMMITTEE

TO HEAVEN AND BACK

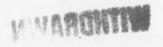

TO HEAVEN AND BACK
THE NEW MORALITY IN THE PLAYS
OF FRIEDRICH DÜRRENMATT

BY

KURT J. FICKERT

THE UNIVERSITY PRESS OF KENTUCKY

LEXINGTON, 1972

Standard Book Number 0-8131-1266-4

Library of Congress Catalog Card Number 72-183353

Editorial and Sales Offices: Lexington, Kentucky 40506

PRINTED IN SPAIN

DEPÓSITO LEGAL: V. 4.366 - 1972

Artes Gráficas Soler, S. A. — Jávea, 28 — Valencia (8) — 1972

CONTENTS

INTRODUCTION

IN THE POSTSCRIPT to his most successful play, *Der Besuch der alten Dame,* Friedrich Dürrenmatt protests that he is not a moralist: "I describe people, not marionettes, an action, not an allegory, establish a world, not a moral such as people at times ascribe to me."[1] The preponderance of his self-analytic pronouncements, however, indicates that Dürrenmatt is, on the contrary, a didactic dramatist whose plays are vehicles for his moral judgments. "Something must happen," he explains in one instance, "which addresses us from the stage, disquiets our conscience, grips us, disturbingly, naggingly, something that destroys the comedy.... In the catastrophe the truth must become apparent." And he specifies pointedly: "One cannot work on language [itself], but only on ideas; one works on ideas through language."[2] Indeed, the concept of the function of the theater which he evolves in *Theaterprobleme,* his contribution to theory of drama, emphasizes the ideational at the expense of the actual by suggesting that the stage exists as a platform for the playwright rather than as a place commanded by actors: "The stage is for me ... an instrument, the possibilities of which I am trying to become acquainted with while manipulating them."[3]

It is clear to most of his critics that Dürrenmatt's plays are an exercise in the development of ideas. The fact that his basic concern is an understanding of morality has been obscured by the apparent

---

[1] Friedrich Dürrenmatt, *Komödien I* (Zürich, 1957), p. 341. Translations are mine, here and throughout.

[2] Friedrich Dürrenmatt, "Rede an die Kritiker," in *Bestand und Versuch* (Zürich, 1964), p. 193; Dürrenmatt cited in Hans Bänziger, *Frisch und Dürrenmatt* (Bern, 1960), p. 191.

[3] Friedrich Dürrenmatt, *Theaterprobleme* (Zürich, 1963), p. 8.

contradiction in his pronouncements on the subject and by the overwhelming ingenuity of his plays. Their manysidedness and dramatic pyrotechnics have assured Dürrenmatt great success (Siegfried Melchinger calls him "the greatest talent in the German theater") and have afforded the plays themselves a multiplicity of critical interpretations. For example, contributors to *Der unbequeme Dürrenmatt,* a collection of essays, regard the plays variously as satire, theological polemic, theater of the absurd, and other literary forms. Despite this diversity, the critics tend to find an underlying unity in all of Dürrenmatt's works. The foreword to *Der unbequeme Dürrenmatt,* by Willy Jäggi, refers, for instance, to the clear and progressive (*konsequent*) nature of his development. Fritz Buri agrees: "This uniformity of Dürrenmatt's theatrical work derives from the fact that ... everything in the final analysis centers around the same theme."[4] The attempt to arrive at a critical appreciation of the plays involves the search for and definition of this common theme.

Proceeding on the basis that the question of morality is central in Dürrenmatt's works, this study examines the plays chronologically, using the versions collected as *Komödien,* and shows the increasingly evident identification of Dürrenmatt's concept of morality with the contemporary relativistic theory of ethics — the "new morality." Characterized by John A. T. Robinson in *Honest to God* (specifically in Chapter 6), it opposes established morality, the long accepted standards of good and evil, a book of rules, and poses in its place one guide to moral conduct, the commandment of love. According to the proponents of this reinterpretation of Christian ethics, relevant to a modern theology in which God is immanent and not transcendent, the quest for right action is the activity that every man engages in in his daily confrontation with the world, with others. A successful resolution of the dilemma of making the morally correct choice in each situation is achieved, in terms of the new morality, by the individual's relinquishing preconceived ideas about the proper behavior under given circumstances and substituting for them openess, a willingness to allow consideration for others, confraternity, love, to be the sole basis for action.

---

4 Willy Jäggi et al., *Der unbequeme Dürrenmatt* (Basel, 1962), p. 37.

Dürrenmatt has acknowledged his adherence to this principle in a lengthy interview which appeared in the *Journal of Modern Literature* (Vol. 1, No. 1). "Love is the highest good," he states unequivocally (p. 103). At one time he planned a *magnum opus,* a keystone to his work, on the subject of the tower of Babel. Although only the first play of a projected trilogy, *Ein Engel kommt nach Babylon,* was completed, Dürrenmatt's choice of this theme is inescapable evidence of his commitment to a consideration of the question of morality; his intent is clear to deal at length with man's grotesque attempt to reach heaven (total good) and the ensuing disillusionment, which leads, so Dürrenmatt concludes, to an understanding of man's relationship to God and the actual nature of morality.

Identified as a moralist by the editors of the *Handbuch der deutschen Gegenwartsliteratur,* Dürrenmatt is analyzed as possessing three outstanding traits, humor, purpose, and the ability to give literary expression to both. His biography makes apparent the origins of these traits. Although he has protested (the need to protest would seem to be another unmistakable characteristic) that he has no biography, that is, that his life has not afforded him with material which lends itself to conversion into confessional literature, the rather placid course of his life has fashioned a mind of inexhaustible inventiveness and wit. Its sharpness was foreshadowed in his grandfather, a political figure of prominence in Switzerland, who was noted for independent thinking and cleverness. In contrast to this life lived in the public eye, Dürrenmatt's father, a Protestant minister, served inconspicuously for many years in the small town of Konolfingen in the canton of Bern, where Friedrich was born on January 5, 1921. Friedrich Dürrenmatt attended the local school, a secondary school nearby (*Großhöchstetten*), the *Gymnasium* in Bern, then the *Humboldtianum* in Bern (also a *Gymnasium*), where he passed the graduating examination. His studies in literature and philosophy at the universities of Zürich and Bern were never completed. For a time in the early 1940s he tried to establish a career for himself in the graphic arts, but in the meantime he had begun writing, completing in 1943 his first play, which remains unpublished and unproduced. Gradually he reached the decision to make his living as a writer; his first published story appeared in 1945 while he was also writing texts for revues in literary cabarets. In

1947, in Basel, his first play to go before the public, *Es steht geschrieben,* was performed. At this point he married and settled down, [5] living first in one, then in another small Swiss town, the unobtrusiveness of his life disturbed only by the continuing appearance of his literary works together with the performance of his plays, which have brought him fame and undoubtedly wealth.

An important factor in this quiet life, along with the questioning and quick-witted mind, inherited perhaps from his grandfather, has been the confrontation with Protestant theology. As a minister's son, reared in piety, Dürrenmatt could not merely accept his faith but had to try to reshape it into something meaningful. Significantly, his career begins with a religious drama, *Es steht geschrieben,* the study of an aberrant Protestant sect, the Anabaptists. Since it is not a strictly historical play, Dürrenmatt can allude to himself in it, and he allows Jan Matthisson, the head of the Anabaptists, to speak directly to the audience as a commentator on the play in the fashion established by Wilder and Brecht: "We consider it our duty to point out that the author of this dubious and historically downright irreverent parody of the Anabaptist movement is nothing else but — in the broadest sense of the term — an uprooted Protestant, marked with the blemish of doubt, mistrustful in the matter of faith, which he admires because he has lost it." [6]

Although Hans Bänziger believes that Dürrenmatt is the representative Protestant dramatist, just as Claudel is the representative Catholic one, [7] Dürrenmatt is not a theologian, and in the above quotation he disavows adherence to the specific tenets of Protestantism. Nevertheless, his acknowledgment of the importance of the religious dimension in man's life and his interest in certain aspects of Protestant faith were established here at the beginning of his work. Central in Protestant theology are the dogmas of the sinfulness of man, and of God's grace, which redeems man in his sinfulness; and Dürrenmatt proceeds in play after play, as this study proposes to demonstrate, to portray the tension between *Gerechtigkeit,* the

---

[5] Dürrenmatt and his wife, an actress, have three children.
[6] Friedrich Dürrenmatt, *Komödien II und frühe Stücke* (Zürich, 1963), p. 48.
[7] Bänziger, p. 136.

judgment of man's sinful nature, and *Gnade,* God's forgiveness.[8] In the course of his playwriting career Dürrenmatt arrived at a resolution of this dichotomy. In the early plays there is only a tentative commitment to an ethic of love which combines the acceptance of guilt with the freedom to act charitably because of the assurance of God's grace. In the character of Übelohe in *Die Ehe des Herrn Mississippi,* Dürrenmatt first symbolized the concept of the "law" of love, a key concept in the Christian teaching of reconciliation between God and man. "For me Übelohe is the Christian," Dürrenmatt told an interviewer.[9] Subsequently, the ethical nucleus of each play is apparent; it is not, however, the Protestant ethic which Dürrenmatt conveys, but an ethic from a Protestant point of view. The question of morality, of good and evil, right and wrong, echoes and reechoes through his plays, rising above the dissonances with which he has orchestrated them. The answer that he at first faintly, then firmly gives is that "the only force which can understand the other [non-self] is love."[10]

---

[8] See Reinhold Niebuhr, *An Interpretation of Christian Ethics* (New York, 1956): "The myth of the Creator God offers the possibilities for a prophetic religion in which the transcendent God becomes both the judge and the redeemer of the world" (p. 34); and "In the thought of Jesus men are to be loved not because they are equally divine, but because God loves them equally: and they are to be forgiven (the highest form of love) because all (the self included) are equally far from God and in need of His grace" (p. 53).

[9] *Journal of Modern Literature* 1 (1970): 104.

[10] Ibid., p. 96.

CHAPTER I

THE FRUSTRATIONS OF GOOD MEN

Es steht geschrieben

DÜRRENMATT CALLED HIS PLAY *Romulus der Große* an unhistorical comedy; similarly, *Es steht geschrieben* (written in 1945-1946,[1] produced in 1947) can fittingly be designated an unhistorical tragedy. The surface plot deals with the Anabaptists' seizure of power in Münster in the sixteenth century and with their capitulation and brutal execution. However, these events are imparted to the audience by the characters as mere information, and the play's real concerns are ideas and attitudes. The characters are hardly involved in history; in a foreword Dürrenmatt carefully explains that he read nothing to assure his play of historical authenticity, although he considered the relevance of the historical situation to the contemporary scene. The persons in the play thus become hypotheses[2] in regard to the theme which Dürrenmatt discovers in the historical event—the morality achieved by good people, living by the letter of the law, transposing heaven to earth, and its failure.

Representing the Anabaptists and their conviction that true believers are to inherit the earth in order to transform it into a heavenly paradise are Knipperdollinck, a rich convert to the sect

---

[1] Elisabeth Brock-Sulzer, *Friedrich Dürrenmatt* (Zürich, 1964) gives 1946 as the author's estimate of the date.

[2] Dürrenmatt's tendency to treat characters as embodiments of intellectual attitudes rather than persons has been extensively noted. See Josef Strelka, *Brecht, Horvath, Dürrenmatt* (Vienna, 1962), p. 138; Christian Markus Jauslin, *Friedrich Dürrenmat* (Zürich, 1964), p. 126; John Gassner, *Theatre at the Crossroads* (New York, 1960), p. 271.

in Münster, and Bockelson, a very poor convert coming from Leyden to Münster, Dürrenmatt makes no effort to identify Knipperdollinck and Bockelson with historical figures; rather the humorous and ominous qualities of the names themselves contribute to the characterization. Thus, Bockelson, historically prominent as an Anabaptist leader, has as a stage figure an aura of evil and distortion about him (*Buckel* means "hunchback"). Along with other protagonists in Dürrenmatt's plays he functions as an outside agent, ruthlessly setting the play in motion when he enters the rigidly circumscribed community of Münster.

The elements of history and theology which Dürrenmatt has omitted—for he has deliberately disavowed that he is either a historian or a theologian—are replaced by ethical elements, although he is also no philosopher. Bockelson, accepted by the Anabaptists of Münster as prophet and king, plays neither role directly but instead plays the hedonistic role, thinking of himself as Solomon. His great scene is an entirely undramatic Rabelaisian dissertation on gourmet food and drink. His main concern throughout the play is acquiring luxuries and women. So much does Dürrenmatt emphasize Bockelson's ethical point of view—pleasure is the sole good in life—that an evaluation of him as a parody of the true believer (for example, Allemann's) seems quite inadequate.

In addition, Dürrenmatt has suggested a union between Bockelson and Knipperdollinck, his philosophic opposite, a duty-bound altruist; this union, represented in the penultimate scene by their dancing together over the rooftops in the moonlight, is more than an expressionistic tour de force. Knipperdollinck is an exponent of the theory that ethical concepts are a priori—*es steht geschrieben,* God-given—, that God has written down the rules in His Bible. Perspicaciously, the Catholic Bishop, the great opponent of the Anabaptists and ultimately victor over them, summarizes for Knipperdollinck the principles by which the good man lives. "Love your enemies as yourself, sell what you have and give it to the poor, and do not resist evil." [3] It is evident that Knipperdollinck's response to this teaching, a life of poverty and good will toward

---

[3] *Komödien II,* p. 37. Reinhold Niebuhr contends that the vow of poverty "probably was not meant as a rule in the thought of Jesus. It was meant rather as a test of complete devotion to the sovereignty of God" (p. 48).

others, is as unavailing as is Bockelson's attempt to discount altruism altogether.

The two protagonists offer, in the final analysis, radically different answers to the problem of giving meaning to life, but both fail to find the affirmation of life that they are seeking and both die by torture. This gruesome symbol for the defeat of the effort to realize the good implicit in life contains, as is usual for Dürrenmatt, an element of parody or ambivalence. *Gerechtigkeit* brings Knipperdollinck to the rack; as he is dying he proclaims the infallibility of God. A negative supposition acquires, therefore, a positive conclusion (or vice versa). Faith in the face of proof which negates that faith is the only true faith. [4] The last words of the play, spoken by Knipperdollinck, are an indication of the grace of God: "The depth of my despair is only a metaphor for your justice,/ and my body lies on this wheel as if in a hollow, which you now fill to the brim with your mercy." [5] So this play by a self-proclaimed doubter ends with the light of truth in its Protestant manifestation, grace, shining through the aura of despair.

The Bishop, who eventually vanquishes both the Anabaptists and the extremes of morality evinced by Bockelson and Knipperdollinck, is a moral touchstone to the others and the voice of hopelessness. He is a morally uncommitted man: he does not censure Knipperdollinck for his apostasy, but rather fortifies him in it. Neither does he reproach Judith (Knipperdollinck's daughter) for her murderous intent toward him but he has her executed for her confession of it. He lives from moment to moment, and Dürrenmatt gives an accurate account of the time he has lived in uncommittedness: ninety-nine years, ninety-nine days, ninety-nine hours. The Bishop's detachment gives him an air of omniscience which is readily identifiable with that of the author. On the whole, Dürrenmatt keeps himself as author of the play in the foreground, allowing his characters to comment on their lives, frequently in the form of direct communication with the audience; his ideational emphasis is thus clear.

Paradoxically, the part which the Bishop undertakes in the sad affair of bringing to an end the government of good people in their

---

[4] See Bänziger, p. 135: "In the parody of faith one senses faith."
[5] *Komödien II*, p. 115.

New Jerusalem on earth does not represent the victory of moral neutralism or of a morally uncommited pragmatism. "There is no victor in this struggle," [6] the Bishop proclaims with an intelligence lacking morality but perceptive enough to recognize its own futility. Nothing has been solved by the rise and fall of the Anabaptists; when the Bishop stands apart and refuses to render judgment, saying, "We can accomplish much good in the world if only we are modest," he approaches the attitude of the author toward his material: "In times of turmoil we appreciate clarity." [7] *Es steht geschrieben* explores moral attitudes without reaching any conclusions, but the ethical considerations are the gist of the play, as Beda Allemann has pointed out in his critique, speaking of its *ethische Vordergründe*. [8]

The need for commitment which Dürrenmatt as yet wishes to deny, has a part, if an obscure one, in the play. Knipperdollinck's daughter Judith holds the center of the stage for a few brief moments. As a woman she is endowed by Dürrenmatt with emotional rather than austerely intellectual qualities. Out of love she follows her father into degradation, gives herself to Bockelson to save her father, and undertakes the murder of Bockelson's oppressor, the Bishop. In the character of Judith, sketchily presented, Dürrenmatt seems to make an overture toward considering the new morality—love as the only viable form of justice (*Gerechtigkeit*). But he ignores, to a large extent, the drama implicit in the role of Judith and lets it end even more inconclusively than the play itself. Other minor roles also add interest to the proceedings without offering additional ethical overtones. For instance, Jan Matthisson, the selfless leader of the Anabaptists, devotes himself with all the intensity of Knipperdollinck to the principle of *es steht geschrieben* —a code of behavior prescribed by the Bible; he goes to his death literally wielding the sword of *Gerechtigkeit,* a battered version of which Knipperdollinck drags with him in his wanderings among the outcasts of society. Matthisson's death and defeat are as cruel as Knipperdollinck's.

---

6 Ibid., p. 114.

7 Ibid., pp. 37, 34.

8 Beda Allemann, "Dürrenmatt: *Es steht geschrieben,*" in *Das deutsche Drama,* ed. Benno von Wiese, vol. 2 (Düsseldorf, 1958), p. 430.

The gloom and sense of tragedy which surround the disastrous consequences of the effort by good men to establish a heavenly kingdom on earth are mitigated by Dürrenmatt's didactic approach to his emotionally charged material. He lets the monk Maximilian Bleibeganz introduce his play with the admonition to the audience: "Preserve the good, forget the mediocre and learn from the bad." [9] Bleibeganz, an early instance of the subtlety and humor with which Dürrenmatt names his characters, escapes death at the hands of the ubiquitous Dürrenmatt executioner, who makes his first appearance in *Es steht geschrieben.*

As yet the lesson to be gleaned from this harvest of frustration remains unclear. Each of the figures in the play responds to his desire to fulfill some purpose, to act on the value he places on life. But despite Knipperdollinck's last-minute cry of hope, the characters in *Es steht geschrieben* leave the good in life a mystery. So Ruth Blinn, considering the question "Is Friedrich Dürrenmatt a Christian writer?" concludes that commitment is lacking: "But this distorted reflecting of the bad and the obscure [*Dunkeln*], into which no light from above shines, is not a Christian, but at the most a moral act." [10]

---

[9] *Komödien II,* p. 18.
[10] Blinn cited in Jauslin, p. 134.

CHAPTER II

TWO GOOD MEN: ONE BLIND AND ONE SEEING

Der Blinde and *Romulus der Große*

THE CONFLICT IN *Es steht geschrieben* between a Don Quixote of morality (Knipperdollinck) and a Don Quixote of amorality (Bockelson),[1] left unresolved, is reexplored in Dürrenmatt's second play, *Der Blinde* (1948), in which the historical has all but yielded to the allegorical. There is the mere suggestion of a historical basis for the events in the play, the Thirty Years War, while the foreground is occupied by symbolic figures of the proportions of Satan and Job. The fact that *Der Blinde* is a reworking of the Job theme has frequently been acknowledged. The man of moral temper, like Job called upon to affirm his belief in a just God and a just creation, is in the paradoxical metaphoric language of Dürrenmatt a blind man. A confrontation between good and evil takes place in the soul of this protagonist, a philosopher-king without a kingdom—actually a duke in devastated Germany, a man of conscience and good will. His adversary, Negro da Ponte,[2] named with Dürrenmatt's usual subtlety, represents the powers of darkness and evil. Da Ponte, champion of an amoral materialism, makes it clear that Dürrenmatt is concerned with a debate on ethics in the form of a play: "The curtain rises," he says, "and you see nothing else but a human being, the (sole)[3] content of my play."[4]

---

[1] Jauslin, p. 68.

[2] The Italian name may indicate a slight relationship to Shakespeare's *Othello;* see Jauslin, p. 128.

[3] A Luther-like insertion.

[4] *Komödien II,* p. 147.

The peace of mind, the inner assurance of the duke is at stake
in a struggle between belief and disbelief. Is his faith in the goodness of God and of life dependent on an illusion so patent that
only a blind man could harbor it? A stranger, da Ponte, whose
ruthlessness is based on his amoral character and lack of responsibility, appears—as will become the custom in Dürrenmatt's plays—
and the attempt at disillusionment begins. Like the plagues visited
on Job, revelations engineered by da Ponte strip the good blind
duke of every comforting belief. Trusting God and lied to by his
retinue, he thinks his country has been spared the devastation of
war, but now he must undertake a mock flight from pursuing armies,
only to be overtaken and confronted by the quasi-god of war,
Wallenstein (actually a black soldier), who mocks him by talking
gibberish.

Like Lear (and the Shakespearean aura of the play is as evident
as the Biblical), the duke feels the lash of the rebelliousness of his
children—a cynical son who holds his father's goodness in contempt,
believing in a world without order or meaning, and a daughter who
lives existentially ("I act as I am.... I am free"),[5] scorning her
father's purposefulness. The duke's children are taken from him:
he himself condemns his son to death for treason, and his daughter
kills herself as a gesture of the meaninglessness of life. But the faith
of the father outlasts the skeptical philosophies of his children. The
existential fervor of Octavia, the daughter, who proclaims that she
has chosen freedom over enslavement to a priori concepts, accepts
the revulsion evoked by the hopelessness of life ("I will accept guilt
and want no mercy"), and carries the banner proclaiming "I fulfill
what I am," is absorbed by the loving solicitude of the father.
Over her body he reaffirms his conviction that goodness prevails:
"You have become my burden, the guilt I bear, the punishment I
suffer, the justice meted out to me, the hope for grace which never
leaves me."[6] The father's faith is also unshaken by his son's fanat-
icism ("What good does it do you to look into the sun unless you
see: sooner or later the sun will die away?"), his blasphemy ("I
am my father's God..., doctor in the field of painful speeches and
thinker of various thoughts"), or his ultimate cynicism ("There is

---

[5] Ibid., pp. 157, 155.
[6] Ibid., pp. 172, 187.

no love"). Indeed the death of Palamedes, the son, is a victory for
the duke: "Like a cloak your guilt now falls from you./ Between
us let there be now only the love which a father has for his son." [7]
Winner in these two minor philosophic skirmishes, the duke has
only an ambiguous kind of success in his struggle against the ab-
stract amoral force represented by da Ponte. Dürrenmatt lets the
devil have the last word in this play, even though the tempter has
to quit the scene and allow the duke to keep his blind faith.

Early in the play the source of contention between the duke and
da Ponte is elucidated. The existence of God which predicates the
existence of the concept of good and evil (that which is ordained
by God and that which resists Him) is the foundation of the duke's
structure of values. "We now pray to God," he says, "in the presence
of all of you, to your and our judge, that faith be given us, which
will divide the night that surrounds us with a sword so that in His
light the good may be separated from the evil." The satanic da
Ponte, identified by Palamedes as a fallen god, states in turn his
amoral purpose in tormenting a blind man: "This is the power
which one man can have over another, proof of the fact that there
are only men and that everything that happens comes from men,
good and bad fortune [alike]." [8] In the end each man remains un-
convinced by the other's arguments. For da Ponte the blind man
has proved nothing but his blindness. The duke stays with his
faith, but in this play it is a faith without an underlying principle:
"Thus we lie broken in the sight of God," he laments, refusing to
continue the struggle with the Adversary, "and thus we live in His
[eternal] truth." [9] Dürrenmatt has written a problem play, to which
a solution, such as that provided by the advocates of the new morality based on the principle of love, is still lacking, although at times
it seems that the answer is imminent.

Dürrenmatt's third play, *Romulus der Große* (written in 1948,
produced in 1949, rewritten in 1958), [10] seems at first glance to be
a deliberate attempt to turn from the type of play which leaves
moral dilemmas unresolved except by death, namely, tragedy. *Rom-*

---

[7] Ibid., pp. 174, 127, 129, 169.

[8] Ibid., pp. 144, 147.

[9] Ibid., p. 191.

[10] *Komödien I* has a new version dated 1964. Bänziger gives the dates
1949 and 1957 for the two earlier versions.

ulus is the first of Dürrenmatt's tragicomedies. Its essence is wit and humor. Inventiveness has replaced the presentation of the problem, as Dürrenmatt states in *Theaterprobleme* in justifying his new approach to the theater. "Tragedy as the strictest of the forms of art presupposes an established order of things in the world.... Tragedy is without inventiveness." [11] Because the modern world lacks all order, it cannot be expressed in terms of the tragic. The critic Walter Jens has confirmed Dürrenmatt's contentions: "Where ... a firmly established order of things is no longer present as a premise, there can be no tragedy." He stipulates further that in tragedy event determines character, whereas in the modern antitragic play character creates event. [12] Thus it is that *Romulus* establishes the modernity of Dürrenmatt and marks his coming into prominence as a playwright of inventiveness, for Romulus the Great is an anti-hero in a play which refuses to provide a tragic denouement to an immanently tragic situation.

History provides the occasion, and nothing else, for Dürrenmatt's first tragicomedy. History has become relativistic; it is no longer established fact. Yesterday is today; yesterday's idiom is today's. Events of the past are as they might be if they were occurring now. Romulus is "the Great" not for his historic achievements, but rather for his lack of them. He is a parody of the tragic hero who dies for his country or his convictions. So fragmented has the modern world become that all philosophic concepts are inadequate; so impersonal has the modern state become that sacrificing one's self for it is inconsequential.

Underneath the innovations in dramatic technique which mark *Romulus* as the first of the tragicomedies persist the moral dilemmas which Dürrenmatt left unresolved in his earlier plays. Despite his urbane manner and sharp wit, Romulus is a serious man, an exponent of a code of morality. In his postscript to the play Dürrenmatt depicts him as sitting in judgment on the world. Specifically, Romulus in his one great achievement condemns the Roman Empire for its lack of conscience: "Rome betrayed itself. It knew the truth, but it chose force; it knew humanity, but it chose tyranny." He has made himself Rome's conscience: "Fearlessly to face things,

---

[11] *Theaterprobleme*, pp. 45-46.
[12] *Statt einer Literaturgeschichte* (Tübingen, n.d.), pp. 88, 106.

fearlessly to do right, I have practiced this art all my life." [13] Thus
Romulus acts with a certain ruthlessness, reminiscent of that of da
Ponte; Allemann describes him as a personification of the lack of
responsibility (*Verantwortungslosigkeit*). [14] His refusal to fulfill his
obligations as emperor is the means to his morally appropriate
ends. He tells his wife, who admits that she married him to become
empress, that he used her in like fashion—but "what was a goal
for you was for me the means." [15] He became emperor only to
execute an act of judgment. Romulus is therefore another version
of the good man; like Knipperdollinck, like the duke, he believes
in a preestablished moral order. Moral values are stable; infractions
of the rules of morality are punishable: such are the tenets of the
faith of this Roman emperor whose aim it is to make himself a
martyr. He will die in the cause of justifying God's ways to man.

But in the light of Dürrenmatt's theories of the drama, the tragic
is unacceptable on today's stage. A reversal of the situation occurs,
therefore, in the last act of the play. Dürrenmatt says in his postscript that now the world judges Romulus. Judgment comes in the
person of Odoaker, the German general whose armies, according
to the plan of Romulus, are to liquidate both the Roman Empire
and its emperor. The German barbarian, however, is an admirer of
the classical world, and he generously sends Romulus into peaceful
retirement instead of to his death. In the meantime, face to face
with an authority who represents reconciliation instead of retribution—a merciful system of morality—Romulus has come to acknowledge his presumptuousness in daring to judge in place of God
(*Vermessenheit*). [16] He is the first of Dürrenmatt's antiheroes to
acknowledge his self-righteousness.

The unacceptability of the Old Testament code of morality (an
eye for an eye) has already been suggested to Romulus in his
dealings with Ämilian, his daughter's fiancé, escaped from German
captivity. The emperor tries to justify his course of action (condemn-
ing to extinction the country for which Ämilian has suffered) to the
young man and fails. Ämilian, Dürrenmatt specifies, is the opposite

---

[13] *Komödien I*, pp. 60, 55.
[14] Allemann, p. 429.
[15] *Komödien I*, p. 50.
[16] Bänziger, p. 141.

of Romulus: "It is his role to see with the eyes of humanity
[*menschlich*]." [17] At the same time Ämilian has to excess the quality
which Romulus so patently lacks, blind love for his country. It is
Romulus who sees that the love between his daughter and Ämilian,
if it exists, is more important than empires. Unfortunately his insight into his daughter does not carry over into the political sphere;
there Romulus insists on justice (*Gerechtigkeit*) instead of love or
mercy. Only in the figure of Übelohe in his next play will Dürrenmatt achieve an amalgamation of the two principles. In *Romulus*
the variety of moral philosophies espoused by the characters in, for
instance, *Es steht geschrieben* is lacking. One of the emperor's
chickens is the only character of note philosophically: the hen that
lays most consistently, Marcus Aurelius, is named after a famous
Stoic. But the human beings who enter into the life of the last
Roman emperor are, in general, players in a farce—theatrically ef-
fective, wittily entertaining, but metaphysically unembellished.

---

[17] *Komödien I*, p. 78.

CHAPTER III

THE MAN UNDER THE NEW MORALITY

Die Ehe des Herrn Mississippi

THE MORAL DEPTH OF ALMOST all the dramatis personæ in Dürren-matt's next play, *Die Ehe des Herrn Mississippi* (written in 1950, produced in 1952), compensates for a certain shallowness in some of the characters in *Romulus*. Dürrenmatt confesses in the play itself that he is concerned primarily with the interplay of ideas; he speaks directly to the audience through Übelohe, a character similar to the commentator in Thornton Wilder's *Our Town:*

> The question might be raised, as to *how* the author took active part in all of this, whether he simply moved from one inspiration to another, or whether some secret plan guided him. Oh, I'll take his word for it that he didn't bring me into being lightly..., that it was a matter of investigating what happens when certain ideas run head-on into people who take these ideas dead seriously.... And this, too: that our inquisitive author was concerned with the question of whether or not the intellect—in one form or another—is capable of changing a world which merely exists without having an idea. [1]

Having explained his purpose through Übelohe, Dürrenmatt proceeds to identify himself with the character who has just been allowed to step out of his part in order to talk for the author: "So this lover of gruesome stories and worthless comedies, who created me, this persistently writing Protestant and hopeless dreamer, had me broken, in order to get at my insides...; so he humiliated me in order to make me not like a saint (saints aren't of any use

---

[1] *Komödien I*, p. 116.

to him) but to make me like him, to interject me in the experiment of his comedy not as a victor, but as a victim, the only state in which man ever appears." [2] *Die Ehe des Herrn Mississippi* leads, therefore, to intimate knowledge of the author's philosophy, but the path to such a revelation is labyrinthine, beset with all the devices available to a master of theatrical technique. This comedy belongs to the theater of the absurd.

Besides being explicator and the sometime *Doppelgänger* of the author, Übelohe is a touchstone for the moral attitudes of the other characters in the play. In this respect Dürrenmatt dismisses the importance of using Mississippi in the title—Übelohe or another name would have done as well. Significantly, however, Florestan Mississippi espouses a moral code which conflicts directly and dramatically with that of Übelohe and the author. The marriage of Mr. Mississippi is intended by the bridegroom to be a triumph of the strictest morality. Paradoxically, Mississippi's morality has already been undermined by the love between his fiancée, Anastasia, and Übelohe. Mississippi's shaky set of values is, nevertheless, based on the most well-founded and clear-cut of all codes of morality, the Mosaic law, which he wishes to reestablish. He is the foremost exponent of concepts of good and evil as expressed in the Bible—God-given, plainly a priori. In the light of Protestant exegesis of the Bible every man who believes in and practices God's word becomes his own judge. Dürrenmatt lets this religious maxim become fact; in an article, "Confessions of a Plagiarist," which he published to disavow any resemblance between *Die Ehe des Herrn Mississippi* and Wedekind's *Schloß Wetterstein,* he identifies Romulus as the model for Mississippi, both being self-appointed judges. As Romulus presides over the dissolution of the guilty Roman Empire, so Mississippi, who has poisoned his adulterous first wife, sentences himself to marriage to a murderess—a marriage which will be both imprisonment and occasion for remorse. As a husband he torments himself and his new wife, Anastasia, and as prosecuting attorney he secures the death sentence for hundreds, even for minor infractions of the law, believing himself to be fulfilling his responsibility to God and man; using the divinely inspired guideline which

---

[2] Ibid., pp. 116-17.

separates right from wrong, he calls himself the completely moral man. [3]

Modern Christian moralists—for example, Bonhoeffer, Bishop John Robinson, and, in this play as well as afterward, Dürrenmatt— attack the presumptuousness, the pride, which lies behind this faith in an aggregate of rules of conduct. Joseph Fletcher, the delineator of "situation ethics," an ethical system based on *agape,* writes: "In this kind of morality, properly labeled as legalism or law ethics, obedience to prefabricated 'rules of conduct' is more important than freedom to make responsible decisions." [4] Mississippi is bound to the past, hypnotized by the preciseness of the written word. Standing in awe of the cogent, the principle of orderliness, he resembles one aspect of his author, Dürrenmatt. [5] Reared to act upon his convictions, Dürrenmatt must find life problematical in the modern world, where convictions are largely replaced by doubt. The dilemma of Mississippi is, therefore, also that of Dürrenmatt; Dürrenmatt resolves it in the character of Übelohe. The attempt to live by preestablished standards of conduct is grotesque, for the root of morality lies in the individual, in his volition, the will to act out of love. "Nothing we do is truly moral unless we are free to do otherwise," states Joseph Fletcher, implying that the basis of ethical behavior is volition. [6]

Irrespective of what he does, Übelohe is a selfless man. He represents the principle of love, not a physical love (compare in this instance Anastasia) but a love centered in the will (*agape*) which engenders moral behavior, that is, the good, without reference to rules of conduct. Because of his selflessness Übelohe is the only character in the play of whom Dürrenmatt fully approves. Thus Übelohe, acting as interpreter of himself and his author, proclaims: "So he [the author] created me, Count Bodo von Übelohe-Zabernsee, the only one whom he loved with a passion, because I alone in this play undertake the [great] adventure of love, this noble ad-

---

[3] Ibid., p. 100.

[4] Joseph Fletcher, *Moral Responsibility* (Philadelphia, 1967), p. 231.

[5] Niebuhr warns: "Orthodox Christianity ... cannot come to the aid of modern man, partly because its religious truths are still imbedded in an outmoded science and partly because its morality is expressed in dogmatic and authoritarian moral codes" (p. 14).

[6] Fletcher, p. 136.

venture, being successful in which or being subjugated in which constitutes the utmost dignity of man." [7] Übelohe—the name, almost translatable as "evil conflagration," is another instance of the paradoxical in Dürrenmatt—loves Anastasia in the first place not only out of a desire to possess her; after she has poisoned her husband, he goes on loving her out of a desire to atone. Doing penance, he wishes to redeem mankind. He explains to Mississippi: "I felt sorry for mankind."

MISSISSIPPI: You loved them all?
ÜBELOHE: All.
MISSISSIPPI: In their grime, in their greed?
ÜBELOHE: In all their sins....
MISSISSIPPI: And what do you get from this love for a woman who doesn't belong to you?
ÜBELOHE: Nothing but the hope that the soul of my beloved will not be lost as long as I go on loving her, nothing but this faith. [8]

Übelohe, the committed Christian, is a forlorn figure in contrast to such activists as Mississippi, the self-righteous executioner, and Saint-Claude, the communist. [9] Dürrenmatt lets Übelohe appear at the end in the guise of a Don Quixote, who closes the play with the idea that life is an unending comedy, lived so that in man's helplessness the glory of God (*Herrlichkeit*) may be reflected. [10] Nevertheless, Dürrenmatt allows Übelohe a kind of triumph; betrayed in his expectation that love, which he equates with truth, will win him Anastasia, he still can give her up with the expectation that love will outlast this and every personal calamity:

ÜBELOHE: Faith is lost....
ANASTASIA: Hope is gone....
ÜBELOHE: Charity alone remains. [11]

---

[7] *Komödien I,* p. 116.

[8] Ibid., p. 136.

[9] Niebuhr explains the relationship between communism and morality thus: "Marxism ... is the perfect product of a naturalistic religion which tries vainly to domesticate the eternal and absolute and to fit the vision of perfection into the inevitable imperfections of history" (p. 26).

[10] *Komödien I,* p. 157.

[11] Ibid., p. 141.

The supposition made by the exponents of the new morality is that this kind of love, charity toward all men, constitutes the only basis for a code of morality. Good comes solely from the exercise of love, the selfless act which allows one human being to accept another (or all others) as he is without reference to preconceived notions of how he ought to be. Therefore justice, previously the result of a moral code, becomes love, now the very form of the moral code. "Justice," Fletcher stipulates, "is love facing the social and circumstantial dimensions of life and history"; and Niebuhr concurs: "The law of love is involved in all approximations of justice, not only as the source of the norms of justice, but as an ultimate perspective by which their limitations are discovered." [12] For Dürrenmatt the philosophic and theological ramifications of the new morality fade into insignificance beside the poetic insight afforded by the concept of all-embracing charity. Dürrenmatt's biographer, Elisabeth Brock-Sulzer, thus summarizes his thinking on the old morality, justice as a reward for good works and punishment for evil, and the new morality, justice as love meted out evenhandedly: "And God is no longer only a vengeful [strafend] God, who may punish, but since this is a matter of the forgiveness of our sins and the peace of our souls, He is a merciful God, who is capable of holding love and justice together in His hand." [13]

Übelohe's "love in spite of everything" [14] is defined in contrast to the kind of love represented by Anastasia. Love as she knows it is only physical and is completely amoral. She lives in existential fervor, only for the moment. [15] Her name, meaning "the resurrected," may indicate the unreflective spontaneity of the life force, for she is unthinking. Ironically, her life ends bitterly because of this quality: she becomes the victim of her own attempt at poisoning. But Übelohe's love prevails. Anastasia, Mississippi (also poisoned), and Saint-Claude (assassinated by his fellow communists) are resurrected from death out of the author's and God's charity.

If Dürrenmatt pairs Übelohe and Anastasia in order to elucidate the concept of love, he puts Mississippi and Saint-Claude together

---

12 Fletcher, p. 78; Niebuhr, p. 128.
13 Brock-Sulzer, p. 251.
14 Der unbequeme Dürrenmatt, p. 27.
15 "Anastasia is a modern [version of] Lulu." Bänziger, p. 146. See also the characterization of Anastasia by Saint-Claude, Komödien I, p. 88.

to emphasize the diametrically opposite concept. Saint-Claude identifies himself and Mississippi as the two greatest moralists of the age. Both seek justice, he explains, but his is a justice of this world, while Mississippi's is transcendent. Motivated by a desire to better mankind, they proceed on the premise that man's situation can be altered—according to Mississippi, by strict adherence to a system of punishments for infractions of the Mosaic law; according to Saint-Claude, by political revolution. Saint-Claude labels his theory of progress as "scientific," Mississippi's as "theological," although he agrees with Mississippi that the basic human flaw is immorality. [16] But their plans go awry; Dürrenmatt confounds them both with the contention "that the conversion [*Veränderbarkeit*] of the world by the individual can no longer be realized, has been placed outside the realm of the possible." Thus the only solution to the moral dilemma in which the world finds itself, knowing good and willing evil, is provided by Übelohe: "In Übelohe faith and love take a stand against the law and deeds [*Werke*]." [17]

In addition to the ethical idealist, Mississippi, and the ethical realist, Saint-Claude, there appears in *Die Ehe des Herrn Mississippi* the amoral pragmatist and unprincipled activist in the person of the government official, *der Minister*. "Ideals are well and good," he concedes, "but I must limit myself to the possible." Skeptical about Mississippi's and Saint-Claude's faith in the betterment of mankind ("Everything in this world can be changed ... but man"), [18] he shares to this extent the viewpoint of Übelohe, and he is the only character in the play who achieves his immediate goal: the government falls into his hands. His successs, however, is transitory; lacking Übelohe's insight into the nature of man's immutability as it is related to the existence of God, the official remains a comic figure without true depth, while Übelohe, despite Dürrenmatt's disclaimer, acquires the stature of a saint or, at the least, that of a truly good man.

All these characters embodying philosophic ideas and ideals are made real by dramatic devices—a clock which acts as a door, a window with a southern or classic view on one side of the stage and on the other side a window framing a northern setting, a table

---

[16] *Komödien I*, pp. 112, 109.
[17] *Der unbequeme Dürrenmatt*, pp. 112, 47.
[18] *Komödien I*, p. 107.

around, under and over which all the action occurs, lowered posters, characters resurrected from the dead, and many others. The New York theater critic Walter Kerr in reviewing a production of the play decried just this juxtaposition of a plenitude of ideas and "immoderately strong theatrical devices." This mixture, however, makes *Die Ehe des Herrn Mississippi* the first play which can be labeled "genuine Dürrenmatt."

CHAPTER IV

IN THE PRESENCE OF GOOD

Ein Engel kommt nach Babylon

DÜRRENMATT'S PLAN TO DRAMATIZE mankind's bold attempt to arrive at the seat of good, the building of the tower of Babel, remains uncompleted except for a reworking in 1953 [1] of a tentative form of the play, a fantasy, *Ein Engel kommt nach Babylon.* Dürrenmatt presents a prelude to the erection of the tower and undertakes to explain man's motivation for storming the heavens. In his paradoxical fashion, the occasion for creating the tower to heaven is heaven's descent to earth in two heavenly creatures incorporating two aspects of the good. There is, first of all, a rather befuddled angel, amazed at the goodness of God's creation. Dürrenmatt does not consider why an angel should not take the beauty of the world for granted since he is concerned with portraying the perfection of the universe strictly in its physical aspect. His angel all but restates Leibniz's theory of the best of all possible worlds: "Whatever is created is good, and whatever is good is happy." [2] Philosophically he appears to represent deism. Again paradoxically, this symbol of God's removal from earth ("It is my duty to leave mankind behind")[3] has as a mission the delivery to mankind of a gift, a symbol of God's never-failing presence on earth. God's loving solicitude for mankind is most clearly expressed in the Protestant notion of grace—redemp-

---

[1] *Komödien I* has a revised 1957 version.
[2] Ibid., p. 165.
[3] Ibid., p. 186.

tion, the evolving of good out of evil [4] — and Dürrenmatt lets a young woman, feeling but unthinking, play the part of God's munificence. Kurrubi (a corruption of "cherub") comes from the hand of God to be placed in the hand of the poorest of human beings, a generosity suggesting the all-embracing quality of God's grace.

Ein Engel kommt nach Babylon exhibits the refusal of most men, absorbed in contemplation of their self-centered goodness, to accept true goodness. The substance of this goodness is, as was the case for Übelohe, love. Kurrubi explains: "I was created out of nothingness so that I might love you for ever and ever." [5] That the nature of this love cannot be understood by theologians bound to the historical approach to religion Dürrenmatt suggests through Utnapischtim, high priest in Babylon. "When I was young and the great flood came, I was convinced," he reveals, "that heaven demanded of man the ultimate.... [Now I am convinced] heaven demands of man [only] the possible. For heaven loves us precisely for our imperfections." Thus he tries to convince Kurrubi, perfect goodness, to compromise by undertaking service to the church and to the state. The dictates of the new morality require, of course, that love should be free, an end in itself, not a means. But the high priest's code of morality is a worldly one; earthly justice and peace—in short, order in the affairs of men—constitute his idea of the good. [6] He shares this concept with the prime minister, for whom the intervention of heaven must have a practical purpose because the world is orderly and logical. The self-righteousness of these men, who cannot accept the incomprehensibility, or inaccessibility, of heaven embodied in the mysteriousness of Kurrubi, is to reappear many times in Dürrenmatt's later plays.

While the high priest and the prime minister are minor figures on the political scene, King Nebukadnezar has a major part in

---

[4] See Dietrich Bonhoeffer, *Letters and Papers from Prison*, trans. anon., rev. ed. (New York, 1967), p. 2: "The great masquerade of evil has played havoc with all our ethical concepts. For evil to appear disguised as light, charity, historical necessity, or social justice is quite bewildering to anyone brought up on our traditional ethical concepts, while for the Christian who bases his life on the Bible it merely confirms the fundamental wickedness of evil."

[5] *Komödien I*, p. 188.

[6] Ibid., pp. 233, 234.

Dürrenmatt's projection of the kind of reception which would be afforded a literal version of God's gift of love. He combines the legalism of Mississippi with the equally moral socialism of Saint-Claude: "I strove for perfection. I created a new order of things. I sought to eradicate poverty. I wished to establish rationality." [7] His sense of morality is based on preconceived notions, established values, and ossified rules of conduct. The prime minister clarifies for him the source of the king's personal and political authority:

PRIME MINISTER: If the definition goes, then the king goes.
NEBUKADNEZAR: Then change the definition.
PRIME MINISTER: Impossible. Otherwise the five hundred thousand paragraphs of the Babylonian law will collapse which result logically from the definition of the king, and we will have pure chaos. [8]

In accordance with Dürrenmatt's mordant wit, *Ein Engel kommt nach Babylon* concerns God's gift of grace attaching itself to this monstrosity of self-righteousness, Babylon's king. The result of the encounter between Kurrubi and Nebukadnezar, his rejection of her, symbolizes man's relinquishment of God's love and forgiveness in order to preserve the morality contained in a man-made, inflexible system of values. As a matter of fact, Nebukadnezar brings to an end his part in the play with a show of defiance; he will dare to vie with God. Which will prove more efficacious in establishing good on earth: a mysterious emanation from heaven or a tower maintaining direct contact with heaven itself? "I am going to counter creation out of nothingness," Nebukadnezar shouts to the skies, "with creation out of the mind of man and will find out which is better: my justice or the justice of God." [9] "Dürrenmatt's play...," the editors of a volume of modern German dramas state, "concerns itself primarily with the relationship between man and the Divine, with the endeavors each side makes to understand and pass judgment on the other." [10]

To the figure of the judge, the role which Nebukadnezar assumes to some extent, Dürrenmatt inevitably adds the figure of the

---

[7] Ibid., p. 245.
[8] Ibid., p. 221.
[9] Ibid., p. 212.
[10] Edgar Lohner and Hunter G. Hannum, eds., *Modern German Drama* (Boston, 1966), p. 389.

executioner. In the moral fable which underlies much of Dürrenmatt's work, the executioner plays an ambivalent part. [11] Obviously he symbolizes death; and death, Dürrenmatt contends, has a bad connotation in the modern world, where dying is no longer personal, just and deserved as the wages of sin, but en masse and without purpose. Only a hangman can personify the anonymity and dismalness of this kind of death. Defiance in the face of a meaningless death will fail, Dürrenmatt suggests, particularly in *Nächtliches Gespräch mit einem verachteten Menschen*; he proposes instead acceptance of death in the only frame of reference meaningful for him, the Christian doctrine of being born in sin and dying as redeemed. These concepts, a *credo quia absurdum*, [12] represent something more than a philosophic system of morality; they bring poetic insight and intuitive response to the problem basic to all literature: death.

In *Ein Engel kommt nach Babylon* the poet (*Dichter*) and the executioner are one, for the beggar Akki acquires the mask and the task of the hangman at a time when he is begging for his life. (The paradoxical elements of the plot are perhaps hyperbolic.) Begging connotes a religious stance, and Akki does not relinquish his profession despite the pressures of reasonableness, although he masks it finally under the pretense of being an executioner. Notably, Luther's last written words describe all of humanity as beggars. [13] In depicting King Nimrod as the footstool of King Nebukadnezar, and/or vice versa, the play suggests that the ancient forms of tyranny survive in the modern state, where man is made comfortable at the cost of enslavement to ritual; he gives up his right to rebel, he relinquishes choice. The beggar alone refuses to conform and in so doing chooses a system of morality in which the sole good is humility, a Saint-Francis-like love of all creatures. Akki thus describes the resultant sense of freedom: "We go in rags for the sake

---

[11] Particularly pertinent to an understanding of the role of the executioner is the radio play *Nächtliches Gespräch mit einem verachteten Menschen,* which Elisabeth Brock-Sulzer calls "perhaps *the* guide for readers of Dürrenmatt" (p. 254). The executioner here represents both an ignoble death and redemption; according to *Der unbequeme Dürrenmatt,* he is a Christ-figure (p. 88).

[12] Bänziger, p. 133.

[13] *Der unbequeme Dürrenmatt,* p. 62.

of the pitiableness of humanity and, in order to glorify freedom, obey no law." This abject state permits him to pose as a hangman, for he can give the only possible answer in the face of death: "Endure shame, go every toilsome way, for time will hide it all away, wild hope, deep love, sorrow and mercy, humanity, under a red hangman's robe." [14]

His standing fast (the real executioner, the Solemn One, tells him that he alone does not change), [15] and outwitting the exponents of divisive creeds make him a quasi-hero — a version of the anti-hero. As such he represents Dürrenmatt's concept of the courageous man. In his *Theaterprobleme* Dürrenmatt evolves his theory of the tragicomedy, true tragedy being excluded from the modern stage because of the incoherence of the times. He argues, however, that a character can achieve some nobility: "It is still possible to show [on the stage] the courageous individual." [16] Being courageous means recognizing one's personal guilt and accepting God's mercy. Therefore, in *Ein Engel kommt nach Babylon,* the beggar Akki alone perseveres, and as he escapes from the insanity of the city [17] he takes with him into the desert a consolation which he does not deserve but which was meant for him all along — Kurrubi, God's grace.

Representing the beggar, the hangman, and the courageous man, Akki has yet another function; in a less direct way he is the author, the poet. The *Weltanschauung* he makes known is not theologically or philosophically precise but is based on the experience of one man — Dürrenmatt — a moralist reared in a Protestant tradition which must be revised and made to apply to the modern world. Since Dürrenmatt is expressing himself through the medium of the stage (hardly through philosophy or theology), the stage direction which ends the play serves to depict the frustration and at the same time the hopefulness of its author: "They [Akki and Kurrubi] disappear in the distance; it may be that a few poets are still following after them, skipping through the sandstorm." [18]

---

[14] *Komödien I,* pp. 183, 218.
[15] Ibid., p. 212.
[16] *Theaterprobleme,* p. 49.
[17] "Babylon stands for the metropolis in general" (*Der unbequeme Dürrenmatt,* p. 132).
[18] *Komödien I,* p. 247.

CHAPTER V

IN THE PRESENCE OF EVIL

Der Besuch der alten Dame

THE AFFIRMATION WHICH APPEARS surreptitiously in the final note to *Ein Engel kommt nach Babylon* has vanished without a trace in Dürrenmatt's next and most famous play, *Der Besuch der alten Dame* (written in 1955, produced in 1956). Despair and hopelessness reign in the town of Güllen (in the Swiss dialect *Güllen* is liquid manure), where the play is set; they are subdued only by the victory of greed in this, one of Dürrenmatt's blackest comedies. Dürrenmatt himself calls *Der Besuch der alten Dame* a malicious play (*ein böses Stück*). [1]

The symbol of the overwhelming evil which has taken hold of Güllen, and by implication the world, is the visitor, Claire Zachanassian. She is no more than half human, with artificial limbs and a heart of stone: "My love could not die. But couldn't live. It became something evil like me." [2] Evident are the beginnings of a petrifaction which will engulf her so that she leaves the stage completely an idol of stone, the product of a code of morality consisting of self-serving laws. Legalism, a mockery of true justice, long before had branded Claire, pregnant with her lover's child, a prostitute; it made her immoral and also rich. "I became a prostitute," she confesses. "The judgment of the court made me one." [3] As the result of a paradox which in this case is life's rather than Dürrenmatt's,

---

[1] *Komödien I*, p. 343.
[2] Ibid., p. 328.
[3] Ibid., p. 279.

Claire's immorality is rewarding; she meets, as otherwise she would never have met, the richest man in the world and marries him. The outcast Kläri Wäscher thus becomes Claire Zachanassian, [4] whose wealth is all-powerful. By achieving this transformation she has come to embody the very system of false values upon which her success is based. It is a code of morality invented and perpetuated by man in a world without God; under it the exercise of power becomes an end in itself, and justice becomes retribution.

Claire's colossal act of vengeance moves like a slow poison through the life of Güllen: she buys the town and makes it destitute; she singles out the townspeople and turns them into puppets, things to be manipulated, victims, as Dürrenmatt describes them in his postscript, "of a total revenge that is as logical as the lawbooks of primitive times." [5] Finally she returns to Güllen to seek out her last victim, Ill — the man she had loved and the father of her dead child. She wants the ultimate in earthly justice: a life for a life. As she herself has profited materially from the judgment of a court which sentenced her to the life of a prostitute, so Güllen is to flourish and its citizens grow wealthy if they will sit in judgment on Ill and, with the same kind of legalism, condemn him to death.

Der Besuch der alten Dame concerns the townspeople's reactions and, of course, most of all, Ill's reaction to this brazen exhibition of the ways of the world, its self-serving system of morality. The nonentities in the town, the impoverished, the scarcely brilliant, lack the patience and insight required to come to terms with the situation; they are capable of facing only the problem of their poverty, ironically the most direct form of injustice. The town's officials and leaders are able to consider Ill's predicament in a more sophisticated fashion. The policeman, to whom he appeals for protection as he begins to see increasing evidence of the town's disposition to accede to the old lady's wishes, responds with a show of bureaucratic, simplistic thinking: "In the final analysis we're bound to the law. . . . The police are here to produce respect for the law, to preserve order, to protect the citizen. They know what their duty is." The

---

[4] "Dürrenmatt derived her name from those of the billionaires Zacharoff, Onassis, and Gulbenkian," Peter Bauland, *The Hooded Eagle* (Syracuse, N.Y., 1968), p. 199. Because it is a Greek name, it also suits Claire in her role of a goddess of fate.

[5] *Komödien I*, p. 342.

mayor, to whom Ill next turns for help, tells him outright that there are no moral grounds for restraining the old lady and adds that, after all, "we live in a legally constituted society [*Rechtsstaat*]." [6]

While the ordinary citizen and the representatives of officialdom might be expected to offer Ill no help and to accept most readily the logic of the old lady's system of vengeance, Ill must hope for sympathetic response from those whose professions require a philosophic attitude. Inevitably, Ill brings his fears to the minister. But the minister is caught up in a system of values which does not apply to any tangible situation such as Ill's. He tells Ill that he must not be afraid of people, only of damage to his soul. Ill complains of the prosperity he sees returning to Güllen, a sign of a society whose ethic takes into consideration only material things, not human relationships. The minister confuses this insight with the "ghost of Ill's conscience"; he is a caricature of the obsession of some Protestant sects with guilt ("Think about the immortality of your soul.... Search your conscience.... Take the path of repentance"), together with their neglect of the key concept of God's grace and their helplessness in the face of reality. Instead of sheltering and comforting him, the minister finally sends Ill away: "Run away," he tells Ill, adding a few words parodying the Lord's Prayer, perhaps Dürrenmatt's most bitter comment in the play — "lead us not into temptation by staying." [7]

While the minister fails Ill completely, the schoolteacher takes a momentary stand against the town and its moral corruption, which will turn men of good will into murderers. He is a humanist: "In the final analysis we do have our occidental principles." For the sake of occidental culture, which has transformed man from a barbarian into an egalitarian, the teacher begs the old lady to give up her bloody mission: "Let this ill-boding thought of vengeance go; do not make us go to extremes. Help [us] poor, weak, but decent people lead a more dignified life. Fight your way through to pure humanity." [8] Claire counters with the contention that in this world only he who can pay is decent. Unable to impress her with the impact of western philosophy on the history of mankind, the teach-

---

6 Ibid., pp. 291, 295, 294.
7 Ibid., pp. 297, 298, 299.
8 Ibid., pp. 306, 308.

er wages a solitary fight against the town's surrender to her bloodthirstiness; he sees her as anathema to the civilized world: "This arch-whore, who changes husbands before our very eyes, shamelessly, who collects our souls." [9] But the intellect alone, which the teacher symbolizes, cannot cope with the problem of separating good from evil; the solution must be intuitive as well as ideational. At the crucial moment, when he intends to confront the world with the truth of the situation in Güllen, he is just drunk enough to take his own safety and well-being into account and to forgo his exposé. Later, at Ill's trial, when the issue has already been decided and humanity has lost to greed, the schoolteacher is afforded a moment of true insight; he seems to speak for Dürrenmatt on this occasion, which, as he explains to Ill, will pass and he will quickly forget. To the townspeople and to the audience the schoolteacher makes clear:

Freedom is at stake here and whenever brotherly love is neglected, whenever the commandment to protect the weak is ignored, whenever marriage is violated, a court deceived, a young mother sentenced to a life of misery. We must simply, in the name of God, take our ideals seriously, dead serious- ly. Riches have some sense only when they lead to riches in mercy: mercy is afforded only those, however, who hunger for mercy. Do you have this hunger for mercy, people of Güllen, this hunger of the mind, and not just this other, this profane hunger of the body...? Only if you do not tolerate evil, only if you can no longer under any circumstances live in an unjust world, may you accept the billion offered you by Mrs. Zachanassian and fulfill the requirement stipulated as to this gift. [10]

The schoolteacher's intelligence only momentarily grasps the truth of the situation and sees a solution. Dürrenmatt's real hero is an anti-hero, Ill. He is a humble man (the name suggests the French *il,* "he," an everyman); he is a shabby, morally ill figure whose life is raised from the humdrum to the symbolic level. Dürrenmatt depicts him as "a simple man who slowly comes to a realization, through fear, through horror, [a realization which is] something extremely personal, [a man] who experiences justice in his person because he admits his guilt, who assumes stature by his dying." [11] Rather a typical member of the community at the beginning of the

---

9 Ibid., p. 317. For some reason, perhaps puritanical, the American version of the play (*The Visit*) omits Claire's proclivity for marriage.

10 Ibid., p. 331.

11 Ibid., p. 342.

play, involved unthinkingly in its inhumane system of values, he finds himself singled out, Job-like, because of his close association with Claire Zachanassian forty years earlier. "To the collective guilt is added the personal guilt of Ill," Fritz Buri notes. [12] Deserted by his fellow citizens, by their officials, by the intellectual leadership in Güllen, and finally by his own family (Dürrenmatt labels them "weak like all of us"), [13] Ill alone confronts the evil in the world, symbolized by Claire Zachanassian and her kind of morality. By accepting the fact of his participation in mankind's wrongdoing, he becomes the courageous man who in Dürrenmatt's view solely deserves the role of the protagonist in contemporary plays.

In addition he acquires a religious dimension: he learns to look upon his own death as an act of atonement. He faces death in the person of Claire Zachanassian, the hangman figure in this play, and conquers it through a belief in its meaningfulness, provided by Christian ethics. "Through [Ill's] struggle with suffering and death," Paul Kurt Ackermann writes, "he becomes a conscious participant in a higher order... [so that] *Der Besuch der alten Dame* resembles to some extent a medieval morality play in which a lesson is demonstrated." [14] Ill, the courageous man, separates good from evil, recognizes the difference between man's justice and God's, and accepts injustice as man's fate when he denies himself God's love and forgiveness. In words which indicate his sense of assurance, acquired not logically but intuitively, Ill describes his readiness to die for his new-found faith: "I shut myself away, conquered my fear. Alone. It was difficult, but now it is done. There is no turning back. You [Güllen] must be my judge. I subject myself to your verdict, whatever it may be. For me it will be justice; what it means to you, I can't know." [15] He has overcome his pride as well as his fear of death, for he had formerly believed that life automatically cancelled out guilt. [16] Only the schoolteacher responds to the lesson in morality provided by Ill's example and understands the humility which Ill has acquired in his triumph over himself. He senses that

---

[12] *Der unbequeme Dürrenmatt,* p. 52.

[13] *Komödien I,* p. 343.

[14] Friedrich Dürrenmatt, *Der Besuch der alten Dame,* ed. Paul Kurt Ackermann (Boston, 1957), p. x.

[15] *Komödien I,* p. 322.

[16] Ibid., p. 342 (Dürrenmatt's postscript).

Ill's ordeal must be the ordeal of all mankind: "I am afraid," he tells Ill, "as you once were afraid. For I know that sooner or later an old lady will come to us, one day, and that then what is happening to you now will happen to us." [17]

Ill's murder, which ends the visit of the old lady, [18] is another ambivalent metaphor in Dürrenmatt's language of the stage, for it represents something positive in a play which began on a note of utter hopelessness. Ill goes to his death not as a victim of earthly injustice but as the recipient of God's grace; Dürrenmatt celebrates here "the victory of grace which has caused [Ill] to walk through hell and in the process to acquire despite all failings [*Versagen*] the gift of being able to persevere." [19] Man's intuitive sense of right, founded on his acceptance of his relationship to a Creator, cannot be effaced, even if it persists only in a few apparently insignificant but courageous men like Ill. "Finally," one critic states in finding a meaning behind the wildly and often bitterly humorous events of this tragicomedy, "the moral foundations of the world [*die sittliche Weltordnung*] are restored in Ill's heart." [20]

In his analytical postscript to *Der Besuch der alten Dame,* Dürrenmatt paradoxically disclaims any purpose other than telling a story on the stage. [21] However, the great international success of the play attests to the fact that, more than any of the earlier plays, *Der Besuch der alten Dame* is a fortunate combination of Dürrenmatt's inspiration, his mastery of theatrical technique and his moral convictions. Bänziger concedes: "The moralist Dürrenmatt, who was much too importunate in *Ein Engel kommt nach Babylon* and in *Nächtliches Gespräch mit einem verachteten Menschen,* retires to the background here." Nevertheless, because of Dürrenmatt's moral earnestness and unfailing capacity to deal with the problematical nature of man's existence in the modern world, *Der Besuch der alten Dame* is "probably *the* tragicomedy of our time." [22]

---

[17] Ibid., p. 318.

[18] Bänziger writes: "Claire Zachanassian symbolizes death for Ill" (p. 176).

[19] *Der unbequeme Dürrenmatt,* p. 55.

[20] Bänziger, p. 205.

[21] *Komödien I,* p. 341.

[22] Bänziger, pp. 176, 171.

CHAPTER VI

IN THE ABSENCE OF LOVE

Frank der Fünfte

THE GREED WHICH PASSES for morality in the modern world has triumphed over good in *Der Besuch der alten Dame.* In it, Bänziger says, "Dürrenmatt measures the vastness of evil against the infinitesimal jewel of virtue." [1] In *Frank der Fünfte,* originally "Oper einer Privatbank" (written in 1958 and produced in 1959), [2] virtue is nonexistent. The world of high finance, where moral qualities labeled good only mask the utmost depravity, serves as a model for the entire civilized world: "The financial institution [Frank's bank] comes to be recognized as a model for the world; the business activities of the employees are made an example of human behavior." [3] Unfortunately, in this instance Dürrenmatt lets his black humor occupy the stage and keeps his ethical probity waiting indefinitely in the wings; Fritz Buri speaks of Dürrenmatt's "undisciplined manner [of proceeding], obscure to the point of incomprehensibility." [4] What results from the lack of depth is to some minds "cabaret theater, too strained satire, an unsuccessful parody of Brecht's *Three-Penny Opera*," [5] or, according to the *Handbuch der deutschen Gegenwartsliteratur,* preciosity. A basic difficulty arises from the fact that the bank's financial problems

---

1 Bänziger, p. 205.
2 Bochum version *(Komödien II),* 1964.
3 Bänziger, p. 184.
4 *Der unbequeme Dürrenmatt,* p. 57.
5 Ibid., p. 6.

motivate the plot, for even when expressed in hyperbolic and consequently comic terms, this kind of subject is undramatic. And yet, although one of the most unsatisfactory of his plays, *Frank der Fünfte* has Dürrenmatt's particular affection; he defends it both in an afterword, "Die Richtlinien der Regie," and in an essay, "Rede an die Kritiker."

Dürrenmatt contends that the moral freedom of the individual is his basic concern in this play. The musical setting even underscores the falsity of the characters' protestations of their good intentions. The introductory song, sung by the head of personnel at the bank, Egli, blandly conveys the dilemma of those caught up in a world in which the only value is monetary: "Man is not free; he exists in the business world."[6] To establish that he is shackled to the convention of making money, Dürrenmatt depicts Egli's betrayal first of his sweetheart, then of his employer, the only people toward whom he exhibits a modicum of warmth; forsaking them, he remains true to the firm, the bank — this is his integrity. The freedom he lacks (Dürrenmatt makes it clear that it is a metaphysical freedom: "He who wants to be free must die")[7] presupposes the making of a choice. The unimpeded exercise of the right to choose is a basic tenet of the ethical system of the new morality: "Nothing we do is truly moral unless we are free to do otherwise."[8] In a crucial scene (Dürrenmatt specifies: "Whoever doesn't understand me in this scene, doesn't understand me at all"),[9] the bank's bookkeeper Böckmann analyzes the freedom of the truly moral person: "At any time we could have turned back, at every moment of our evil lives. There is no legacy that cannot be nullified; there is no crime that must be done. We were free, false priest [Frank], created free and allowed to be free."[10]

The enslavement into which all the characters in *Frank der Fünfte* have fallen results from adherence to standards of conduct, moral guidelines, inherited from father to son; thus Frank is *der Fünfte,* although his Christian name is, with "Dürrenmatt's delight

---

6 *Komödien II,* p. 199.

7 Ibid., p. 282.

8 Fletcher, p. 136.

9 "Rede an die Kritiker," p. 194.

10 *Komödien II,* p. 252.

in fanciful names," Gottfried.[11] Egli notes some of the values society has cherished generation after generation and comments on the kinds of immoral citizens they have produced: "Conscientiousness [*Pflichtbewußtsein*], you cheats; spirit of brotherhood, you rascals; sense of responsibility, you murderers!"[12] Frank's unscrupulous son Herbert (later Frank VI) also contributes to an understanding of the way in which venality masquerades as morality: "Integrity is no aspect of the inner life, rather an aspect of organization. To attain it a much greater ruthlessness is required than in practicing immorality [*das Schlechte*]; only bona fide cheats and rascals [*Schufte*] are capable of achieving the good."[13] Herbert has saved the bank by blackmailing his father and mother; so, Dürrenmatt implies, a man today sacrifices himself and all personal allegiances for the sake of the institutions which maintain his security and keep him physically comfortable.

In *Frank der Fünfte* the bank symbolizes the entire capitalistic world through an institution which is particularly notorious in its Swiss form; the affinity of Dürrenmatt's work with the Swiss scene is generally apparent, as, for example, in his use of the theme of marriage to represent social interaction, the theme of war being inappropriate for a Swiss writer. Loyalty to the bank is shown in *Frank der Fünfte* to be the highest virtue, the equivalent of, if not far above, patriotism and family loyalty. Business ethics require strict adherence to standards of behavior, the rightness or wrongness of which is predetermined by their supposed efficacy, their capacity to produce a profit. The end justifies the means, Dürrenmatt says in his analysis of the character of Frank's wife, Ottilie.[14] "In this kind of morality," Joseph Fletcher proposes, "obedience to prefabricated 'rules of conduct' is more important than freedom to make responsible decisions."[15] Lack of responsibility in this sense has been one of Dürrenmatt's chief criticisms of contemporary society, voiced consistently in play after play, according to Beda Allemann's article on *Es steht geschrieben*.

---

11 Brock-Sulzer, p. 212.
12 *Komödien II*, p. 247.
13 Ibid., p. 273.
14 Ibid., p. 281.
15 Fletcher, p. 231.

There are several attempts in *Frank der Fünfte* to escape the yoke of legalism and to act in freedom — to choose to do the right thing out of love. All fail. Frank V himself tries to take refuge in literature, in a realm of high, untainted ideals. Feeling the need to turn his back on the bank ("I am not a bank director; I am unfortunately a thoroughly good human being"), [16] he flees (cf. Dürrenmatt's "Die Richtlinien der Regie") to Goethe and Mörike; one would like to add Stifter, who is briefly mentioned in *Der Besuch der alten Dame*. But Frank is using the intellect only as a means; he seeks to placate the will, which innately wants to enter into the process of choice, to assume responsibility. It is Frank's bookkeeper Böckmann who makes a genuine effort to break free of the chains of rules, to be responsible to himself. Dürrenmatt thus describes the encounter between Böckmann, who, dying of cancer, repents of his sins (immorality), and Frank, who is disguised as a priest: "The man for whom the intellect is an instrumentality through which release is achieved [*Genußmittel*] meets the man who is looking for the intellect out of his [deep] despair." [17] But Frank cannot allow Böckmann to exercise free will because a precedent would be set which would undermine the base of orderliness upon which the natural world rests. For Dürrenmatt the confrontation between Frank and Böckmann has immense significance: "In the Böckmann scene unjustified hope, unjustified freedom, and the unjustified intellect are opposed by authentic hope, authentic freedom, and the authentic intellect." [18] In a world where, according to Protestant belief, sin will always prevail (even the new morality must make this reservation), Böckmann's plea that he be set free, that he be allowed to die at peace with himself and with God, must be denied. He is murdered before a real priest can hear his confession. Pointedly, Böckmann's name contains the element *Bock*, "scapegoat."

Frustration also comes to Egli, the devoted hear of personnel; but it is the result of his refusal to rid himself of his rage for order rather than the opposite, as was the case with Böckmann, who wanted the freedom of the unknown, the irrational. Chance, a missing link in the chain of cause and effect, confronts the believer in

---

[16] *Komödien II*, p. 225.
[17] Ibid., p. 281 ("Richtlinien der Regie").
[18] "Rede an die Kritiker," p. 194.

a structured universe and leaves him beaten. Egli's moneymaking schemes unaccountably go awry; "chance, the unpredictable, is the greatest enemy [of the charlatan]." [19]

As defeated as Egli in his pursuit of money to save the bank, a "good" cause, is Ottilie, Frank's wife; she also has the bank's interests in mind and at heart. Her solution to its financial difficulties involves the hiring of a prostitute in the service of the bank. Dürrenmatt here employs a literary device of which he is fond, the prostitute as a symbol of the depravity of society: the old lady, Mr. Mississippi's wife, and the blind duke's daughter are all prostitutes. Behind the obviousness of using perverted love as a prime example of the corruption of the soul, there may be a philosophic implication in the prostitute figure. Luther identifies reason as a whore, incapable of love; and Fletcher points out "the single-minded irrationalism of the Luther dictum." [20] Love, according to the new morality willed without reason, not as affection but as open-mindedness, is the only basis for a morality which is not to be perverted by the necessity of conforming, of submerging the individual in a stagnating society. In *Frank der Fünfte* love is strictly physical and commercial. The bank's official prostitute, Frieda Fürst (an extreme example of hyperbole in the naming of characters), describes the nature of love in the modern world: "Love, Señor, makes harsh demands: that is all that I can say. And everybody gets the best price he can when he gives himself away." [21] Frieda's services are repaid by a speedy execution, and Ottilie is forced to look for a replacement. The applicant for the position is Ottilie's daughter, whom she has reared to be a good person — paradoxically, by conspiring to commit every conceivable crime.

In a logically hopeless situation Ottilie turns to the only real hope, God's judgment and forgiveness. She demands judgment, justice, and punishment of the head of state who has jurisdiction over the bank and its employees — Traugott von Friedemann — ironically, the name of a blind and unfeeling tyrant. He cannot comply, he suggests; if he did, the structure of the world [*Weltordnung*] would crumble. "Expect no judgment, expect no justice,

---

[19] *Komödien II*, p. 282.

[20] Fletcher, p. 18.

[21] *Komödien II*, p. 223.

expect no punishment. They would be all too warm and human for the icy world of integrity to which I now send you back. Expect only God's mercy." [22] By denying Ottilie salvation at his hands, Traugott von Friedemann sets in operation the great paradox of God's love: it can't be given, for it already has been given; it can't be deserved; therefore only the undeserving have it. It is the foundation of a system of morality which has no laws, which treats good as a relative value (at times the equivalent of evil, constituting in this respect the cornerstone of situation ethics). In the darkness in which the light of God's grace is only imminent, the play ends.

"In *Frank der Fünfte* there is no longer any saved person [*Begnadeter*], but by considering those who are lost [*die Unbegnadeten*] we can imagine what salvation [*Gnade*] might be like," Werner Oberle contends. [23] This ambiguity, the result of a commitment to morality which never exhibits itself (its presence is felt in its total absence), has made *Frank der Fünfte* an unsatisfactory play according to the critics. But Dürrenmatt insists that the caricatures of people he presents as characters and the Gothic horrors he assembles for his plot are a meaningful comment on life, which he can authoritatively make as "an observer of people and himself." In his afterword to the play the moral fervor crowded offstage by the absurdity of character and event finally appears: "But we all want the good as do Frank's employees: [that is,] happy children, a house in the country, being respectable. Let us be on our guard that we do not merely sing about the good as [my characters] do.... Propriety is more than a nice sentimentality; humaneness is more than a phrase: [they are] a daring venture and lest this daring venture be foolhardiness, we must all be diligent." [24] The dichotomy which is apparent whenever Dürrenmatt analyzes his own work asserts itself in the "Richtlinien der Regie," too, but in this instance his insistence upon being merely a playwright with bright ideas [*Einfälle*] is neatly in balance with his insistence upon having something ethically pertinent to say. He concludes: "In the long run I am a writer of comedies, and if at times I am also a moralist, I am only supplementally so, as an interpreter of myself." [25]

---

[22] Ibid., pp. 277, 278.
[23] *Der unbequeme Dürrenmatt*, p. 23.
[24] *Komödien II*, p. 282. See Bonhoeffer, pp. 7-9: "Of Folly."
[25] *Komödien II*, p. 282.

CHAPTER VII

THE WISDOM WHICH TRANSCENDS

Die Physiker

THE ENCOUNTER BETWEEN the intellect which constructs its own idealistic (and false) world and the intellect which recognizes its limitations, its "guilt," portrayed in *Frank der Fünfte* as the confrontation between Frank and Böckmann, is further elucidated in Dürrenmatt's 1961 play, *Die Physiker*. In singling out the world of science and especially the field of physics, Dürrenmatt hit upon a dramatic metaphor particularly apt for the development of "his basic concerns which always remain those of a moralist." [1] Once again he analyzes good and evil with the result that the paradoxical nature of moral truths becomes evident: an act, such as that of Möbius, characterized as the greatest physicist of all time — his withholding information which could lead to the blowing up of the world — though demonstrably well-intentioned and good, is shown to be intrinsically evil, prideful, and destructive.

Appended to the play are twenty-one aesthetic and metaphysical maxims; in number nineteen, Dürrenmatt calls attention to the fact that reality or truth appears always as a paradox. [2] In number thirteen he isolates the realm of physics as one in which the ambivalence of truth is inescapable. By the ingenious device of having "Newton" and "Einstein" appear onstage, he covers the development

---

[1] Friedrich Dürrenmatt, *Die Physiker,* ed. Robert E. Helbling (New York, 1965), p. xii.
[2] *Komödien II,* p. 355.

of physics and with Möbius, his own invention, projects it into the future. [3] His attack on the moral probity of all physicists is especially pertinent because physics in particular among the sciences has established the mechanistic or "natural" concept of the universe, according to which a system of laws prevails everywhere, in heaven and on earth, and is accessible to man through logic. Rationality is the pursuit of Dürrenmatt's three physicists in their moral as well as their scientific endeavors. Newton confesses his need for order: "I can't stand disorder. I actually became a physicist out of a love for orderliness." Möbius has indeed made the ultimate scientific discovery, the law upon which all other natural laws are based: "The system of all possible discoveries has been closed out.... And now everything is in order." [4]

Möbius's application of his concept of logic to the moral sphere — his keeping safe from a wicked mankind his solution to all the problems of the physical universe by disguising himself as a schizophrenic fit only for an asylum — sets the plot of *Die Physiker* in motion. Various onslaughts against Möbius's castle keep, Fräulein Doktor von Zahnd's hospital for the insane, are discovered and warded off. One of the most vigorous of these assaults is made by Möbius's two fellow physicists and inmates. The delusion that they are Newton and Einstein has brought them into the presence of a physicist greater than they, one who admits to hearing the voice of King Solomon; stripping themselves of this pretense, they prove to be just as rational as he really is. Agents of capitalism and communism, they have crept into Möbius's retreat in order to buy him out. Their efforts at persuasion are loaded with the false kind of logic and morality which Dürrenmatt wishes to expose. "Newton," actually Beutler, tries to justify his proposal that Möbius allow the capitalist nations to exploit his discovery of the law that governs all matter: "It is a matter of the freedom of science and nothing else.... I know people talk today about the responsibility of physicists. All of a sudden we are concerned with fear and are turning moralistic. That's nonsense. It's our job to do pioneering work and

---

[3] Möbius is the name of an actual astronomer and mathematician. Although he is hardly Dürrenmatt's Möbius, the name itself is therefore not without significance.

[4] *Komödien II*, pp. 294, 315

nothing else." [5] Beutler's opponent in the struggle for Möbius's commitment, "Einstein," actually Eisler, a communist, [6] uses persuasion which is equally logical: "But we mustn't exclude [the idea of] responsibility. We are putting powerful means of control in the hands of humanity. This gives us the right to state our conditions. We must be important politicians [*Machtpolitiker*] because we are physicists." [7]

Möbius immediately sees through both of these specious arguments: "We must not let ourselves be led by opinions, but [only] by logical conclusions. We must try to find the rational [answer].... Our goal is the advancement of physics, and yet you [would] deny it [a sense of] responsibility, Kilton [i.e., Beutler]. On the other hand, you, Eisler, [would] obligate physics in the name of responsibility to the power politics of a particular nation. Now let us see ... what is reality." At this point Möbius explores his reasons for concealing himself in a madhouse and depriving the world and his fellow physicists of his discoveries. He fears that such knowledge is deadly. "There is for us physicists only surrender in the face of reality.... We must take back our knowledge." So he has acted out of a sense of moral obligation; responsibility forced him to proceed as he did. "Reason [*Vernunft*] required me to take this step." The moral grounds for Möbius's self-sacrifice are based on a rationalistic, naturalistic system of values; it is the categorical imperative which functions as an appendage of the human intellect and not some transcendent authority which has made Möbius a recluse in an insane asylum. He demands adherence to the same moral principle from his companions; they, too, must act for all physicists. "Either we stay in a madhouse, or the world will become one." Einstein's response to Möbius's plea that the three physicists remain incarcerated has a moralistic tone: "I am a decent person. I'll stay. In honor of you, Irene, and your devotion, I intend to act rationally." [8] (Irene, whose name means "peace," is a nurse whom Einstein has killed to prevent disclosure of the ruse he employed to enter the

---

[5] Ibid., p. 338.

[6] Coincidentally, there was a modern German composer of some repute with communist leanings named Eißler.

[7] *Komödien II*, p. 338.

[8] Ibid., pp. 341, 342, 343, 344.

asylum.) When Newton, too, agrees that logically he must keep on pretending to be insane, the scene ends on a note of ritualistic self-sacrifice:

MÖBIUS: Let us have Solomon [the manifestation of Möbius's madness] appear.
NEWTON: Insane, but wise.
EINSTEIN: Captive, but free.
MÖBIUS: Physicists, but innocent. [9]

The figure of King Solomon, which plays a part in the physicists' rites of immolation, symbolizes the morality of Möbius's action and also obviously symbolizes wisdom; but it is a wordly wisdom which does note exclude the possession of earthly goods. That this kind of wisdom and wealth, obtained by the advance of science, is inadequate in the face of the needs of humanity as a form of life (an expression of God's creativeness and love) Dürrenmatt makes clear from the start. The critic Oberle has pointed out that the two parts of *Die Physiker* cannot be separated into a madcap (*toll*) beginning and a moralizing conclusion but are equally ambivalent (or grotesque). [10] From the first, Möbius speaks of Solomon as a pitiful king: "Naked and stinking he squats in my room as the poor King of Truth, and his psalms are terrifying." [11] Later Möbius recites one of the songs of his mentor, chilling verses about the ultimate achievement of science, the exploration of space, depicted as the wanderings of all but dead human beings through an infinity of dead matter. The substitution of such a belief in man's wisdom for a belief in the mystery of God, Dürrenmatt contends, has disoriented mankind. In his book on Dürrenmatt, Hans Bänziger analyzes the religious aspect of this point of view:

Pious faith ... has given way to fear, in the light of which the Last Judgment means only the end ... which, thanks to the atom bomb, will be followed by nothingness, the senseless circling of a burnt-out planet around a sun turned [completely] indifferent.... Thus what was revelation has become event, but it is no longer a struggle between good and evil.... Mankind as a whole has become guilty, and each one [of us] wants to save not only his ideals but also their opposites: freedom and business-as-usual, justice and tyranny. [12]

---

[9] Ibid., p. 344.
[10] *Der unbequeme Dürrenmatt*, p. 18.
[11] *Komödien II*, p. 312.
[12] Bänziger, pp. 202-03.

In *Die Physiker* Möbius's belief in King Solomon — his faith in
the ability of human intelligence to initiate moral actions — is
crushed by the intervention of Fräulein Doktor von Zahnd, the
director of the asylum, who usurps for herself the concept of King
Solomon and magnifies it so that its true monstrosity becomes apparent. Also in the service of Solomon, she has stolen Möbius's
secrets so that she can make use of the insights of pure science in
engineering space explorations and atomic wars — for her own
satisfaction. The word *Zahnd* refers to "teeth," [13] and Zahnd becomes a symbol of the moral aspect of the scientific materialism
represented by King Solomon: "a principle determining the course
of events [*weltbestimmend*], ... the incarnation of evil bound up
with absolute power." [14] To a certain extent the greedy psychiatrist
is also that anathema to true justice embodied in so many of
the dramatis personæ in Dürrenmatt — the purveyor of a strict
legalism, the advocate of man-made laws elevated to the rank of
universal laws, like Mississippi and the characters in *Frank der
Fünfte*. Accordingly Zahnd is identified by Josef Strelka as an
"expression of the most grandiose mediocrity [*Weltspießertum*]." [15]
For Elisabeth Brock-Sulzer, she is more than an agent of the plot:
"She plays the role of lethal chance." [16] In his explanatory notes
to the play, the "Twenty-one Points," Dürrenmatt defines chance
as the element of the unknown, the unforeseeable which always
crosses the path of calculating people and cancels out their painfully
careful reckoning. So, by committing himself to the asylum and the
care of the Fräulein Doktor, Möbius has miscalculated and has
delivered up his most sanguine ambition, saving the world from
atomic explosion, to utter frustration.

The element of chance, so unacceptable to the rationalist, has
another dimension for the transcendentalist: it functions in the
natural world as does grace in the realm of the authentic intellect,
the realm, perhaps, of the soul. Möbius seems not to have reached
this level of true morality with his personal "tower of Babel"; the

---

[13] Romulus says, "I will seize you with the teeth of justice" (*Komödien I*,
p 61). "The teeth of justice" is Biblical phraseology.
[14] Jauslin, p. 117.
[15] Strelka, p. 119.
[16] Brock-Sulzer, p. 123

workings of divine and therefore perfect justice are not conspicuous in *Die Physiker*. Strelka contends that there can be no doubt that the otherworldly [*das Irreale*] is fundamentally involved in Dürrenmatt's plays, and he believes that the tenor of *Die Physiker* reflects "the greatest moral, indeed religious seriousness." [17] The affirmative aspect of the sacrifice of Möbius, who would seem to have no course open to him but that of resignation to defeat, [18] is indirectly expressed.

The first confrontation between Möbius and a force which could destroy his façade of madness, a visit from his family, is also his first encounter with true humility and goodness. For his wife has remarried and has brought their children and her new husband to bid Möbius farewell; they are bound for the Marianas. The names of the family all have a Christian orientation: Möbius's former wife is Lena (Magdalena), her new husband is the missionary Rose (suggesting Luther's rose, the symbol of his faith), the children are Wilfried-Kaspar (Wilfried suggesting "want peace," Kaspar traditionally one of the wise men), Jörg-Lukas (Saint George and Saint Luke), and Adolf-Friedrich (paradoxically, two tyrants posing as saviors). Möbius recalls taking his son by the hand across Saint Joseph Square. That Möbius stands in the presence of practitioners of the Christian doctrine of love, which they apply to every situation, even encountering a raving relative in a madhouse, is made doubly clear by Rose's readiness with apt Biblical quotations, Frau Rose's loving solicitude, and the children's gesture of affection—they perform a musical piece for their father; these ministrations almost cause Möbius to break down. He steels himself by reciting his wicked "Song of Solomon" and thus avoids giving himself away. No sooner has he disposed of one mystical intrusion on his intellectual self-sufficiency than he must deal with another. His nurse, Sister Monika, with whom he has fallen in love, appeals to him, for the sake of a life together, to abandon his mission to save mankind. "Frau Rose and the nurse Monika represent in their own homespun, philistine ways the 'grace of love' visited upon Möbius," Helbling says. [19] The only logical way which occurs to Möbius to

---

[17] Strelka, pp. 135, 151.

[18] See *Der unbequeme Dürrenmatt*, p. 21.

[19] *Die Physiker*, p. xxviii.

put aside this temptation to let love prevail, while ignoring the "right" thing to do, is to remove that tempation altogether; he murders Monika.

With the vanishing of Monika and the Roses, there remains onstage only one person capable of a faith deep enough to accept love as a standard for moral action: it is Möbius himself who, paradoxically, has just sacrificed himself and his sweetheart to a belief in man as morally superior to God. In his last speech, the closing lines of the play, Möbius experiences a breakthrough, making the leap of faith: "I am poor King Solomon. Once I was immeasurably rich, wise, and god-fearing. Before my might the powerful trembled. I was a prince of peace and justice. But my wisdom destroyed my reverence [fear of God], and when I no longer feared God, my wisdom destroyed my riches." [20] At this moment Möbius has lost his pride, has accepted his sinfulness and has seen through the shallowness of a morality based upon the idea of efficaciousness. Summarizing his conclusions, Strelka states: "Dürrenmatt is certain that man as an intelligence [*ein Wissender*] [in the golden cage] must fail. What follows from this [assumption]? The requirement that he must not take up a disguise or go into hiding? The requirement that he must not be a physicist? Instead of this: the requirement that he must not believe poor King Solomon, but must believe Him who was before, the prince of peace and justice, whose truth never destroyed reverence." [21] Buri also finds in Möbius's last words an acknowledgment of the workings of God's grace, His love. [22] And Helbling depicts Möbius as at least seeming " 'to show the way' to responsible action." [23] Möbius's commitment to responsible, that is, moral, action brings the curtain down on a play which seems a counterpart to its immediate predecessor. Instead of the immorality of *Frank der Fünfte* there is here a struggle for true morality and a victory for it; instead of a plot with baroque proclivities and an insistence upon hyperbole there is the simplicity and dramatic drive of a mystery story; instead of music, the three

---

[20] *Komödien II*, p. 351.
[21] Strelka, p. 157.
[22] *Der unbequeme Dürrenmatt*, p. 61.
[23] *Die Physiker*, p. xxi.

unities. The invincibility of legalism as a system of morality, established in *Frank der Fünfte,* has yielded in *Die Physiker* to the prospect of the emergence of the new morality with its matrix of love: "the only ethic which offers a point of constancy in a world of flux and yet remains absolutely free for, and free over, the changing situation." [24]

[24] John A. T. Robinson, *Honest to God* (Philadelphia, 1963), p. 115.

CHAPTER VIII

THE MYTH OF THE GOOD MAN

Herkules und der Stall des Augias

THE PARADOXICAL NATURE of truth, even the truths discovered by physicists, is one of the tenets of Dürrenmatt's philosophy, codified in the "Twenty-one Points to *Die Physiker*." In literature the need to reflect the ambivalence of reality leads to the employment of myth, which is uninhibited by the laws of logic. Dürrenmatt, whose plots and characters from the beginning have had mythological propensities, devoted an entire play in 1963 [1] to the exploration of one of the myths concerning the labors of Hercules, developing it along the lines of his personal philosophy. He introduces this play, *Herkules und der Stall des Augias,* accordingly: "We present no realistic play, we come [to you] with no thesis play [*Lehrstück*] and even leave the theater of the absurd out of the picture, we present a poetic [*dichterisch*] play." [2]

The fact that the setting for every play of Dürrenmatt is "a world in decay" [3] makes his selection of the country of Elis, where the manure is stacked to the skies, obvious. Elis, in Dürrenmatt's play, has some of the characteristics of Switzerland; it is, if paradoxically untidy, bucolic, democratic, and bourgeois. Its citizens are about as unperspicacious as those of Güllen in Switzerland. Phyleus (Greek for "line of descent"), son of the "President" of Elis, describes his upbringing as being in the middle-class tradition: "I grew up

---

[1] Originally a 1954 radio play, published in 1959.
[2] *Komödien II*, p. 362.
[3] *Der unbequeme Dürrenmatt*, p. 12.

like everybody else in Elis. Tough, sturdy, taking my lickings and handing them out." [4] But his father, Augias (or Augeas), is a good man, a reasonable man. It is he who sees the necessity of cleaning up Elis, of sweeping away the mass of debris which marks the path of humanity in time. Only heroic action can accomplish the task; so the greatest hero available, Hercules, is called upon to stem the tide of waste.

Dürrenmatt's comic portrait of Hercules is conceived of in terms of paradox. A reluctant hero, an unhappy man, an inadequate lover, he represents nevertheless a great ideal and its fulfillment. His mistress, Dejaneira, realizes that the man whose frustrations she knows so well functions as a symbol: "You are a hero," she says, "and I love you. But then I ask myself whether you aren't more of an ideal for me, just as I am an ideal for you." For Augias, believing initially in man's ability to effect the great change in himself from indifference to rectitude, Hercules is "the great opportunity which comes and [then] goes." He looks upon the arrival of Hercules among the Epeians to rid them of the results of their moral sloth as an occasion for resurgence: "The [Epeians] have been given a great opportunity to put their country in order. They must see to it themselves if they know how to make use of this [once-in-a-lifetime] chance." Although Hercules has little feeling for "these well-fed, contented middle-class citizens" whom he is to help purge of smugness, he cannot suppress a sense of mission. He tells Dejaneira, who knows the beauty of the earth and of life: "I will take it upon myself to move mountains of garbage, to do the awkward job that only I can do, but you will give this transfigured [purified] country its plenitude, its spirit, its beauty, its meaningfulness. So we are both a necessity for Elis, both the opportunity for this country to humanize itself." [5]

The time for a change among the Epeians comes and goes, without effect. In Dürrenmatt's version of the legend bureaucracy defeats Hercules. Augias accepts in the end, as Dürrenmatt does, the inappropriateness in modern times of outside forces' (in this respect Hercules is a Dürrenmatt motif) bringing about social and

---

4 *Komödien II,* p. 390.
5 *Komödien II,* p. 403, 426, 397, 384, 404.

ethical change. After Hercules has been removed, Augias reveals to his son, in an act of love and mercy, the only garden in Elis. He explains to Phyleus, at the moment a kind of Candide, that only the individual by himself can act effectively in attaining moral goals for mankind: "Politics never accomplish the good, if we ourselves don't do the good. I changed manure into humus. These are difficult times when one can do so little for the world, but this little we should do at least: [make] our personal effort [*das Eigene*]. The coming of grace so that our world should appear brighter you cannot force to happen, but the prerequisite, this you can fulfill, so that mercy—if it comes—can find in you a clear mirror for its light."[6] That Phyleus turns his back on his father's philosophy (and garden) and chooses to see as reality only the evil in the world, the manure never-ending, is Dürrenmatt's signature to a comedy which is, like all his comedies, a tragicomedy.

But Dürrenmatt's protagonist in the play is Augias, not Phyleus. His garden is the symbol that identifies the courageous man; like Ill in *Der Besuch der alten Dame,* he shows that basically Dürrenmatt believes in "courage, manliness and the power of invincible hope."[7] The purveyor of this creed is the moral man, the good man. In a moment of perspicacity Hercules, himself only a part-time hero and more accurately a part-time circus strong man, depicts the moral man for the "President's" daughter, who fancies herself in love with a legend, Hercules, and doesn't know a false ideal from true goodness: "Sometime or other you will fall in love with a real man, a man who is a true hero, who is afraid as all people are afraid and who overcomes his fear, and sometime or other you will have sons and daughters who love peace and who find all these beasts with which I have to contend to be nothing but fairy tales: and this alone makes it worthwhile to be a man [*ist menschenwürdig*]."[8] So the first series of plays by Dürrenmatt, collected under the rubric *Komödien,* ends with a play in which the injustice brought about by men and their legalism[9] is contrasted with the justice, only

---

6 Ibid., p. 428.
7 Bänziger, p. 204.
8 *Komödien II,* p. 410.
9 See the speech on justice by Polybios, Hercules' secretary: ibid., p. 422.

vaguely hoped for, which comes to those who, conscious of their blasphemy, descend the tower of Babel and accept God's mercy waiting below. In this context Fletcher explains: "Justice and its steward, law, are love (or 'grace') facing the fact that absolute love has to be served relatively, shared and balanced among many neighbors." [10]

---

[10] Fletcher, p. 176.

CHAPTER IX

DESCENT FROM HEAVEN

Der Meteor

THE MYTHOLOGICAL IN *Herkules und der Stall des Augias* has changed, only in degree, into the legendary in Dürrenmatt's next play, *Der Meteor* (1964). [1] The protagonist, a successful writer whose importance the Nobel Prize Committee has acknowledged by awarding him its accolade, is cynically and paradoxically enough a modern "saint," the vessel of a miracle wrought by God. [2] He dies several times over and is resurrected forever and ever. But he is never re-born, and in this respect Dürrenmatt's ethical approach to the (theatrically) absurd plot he has devised comes to the fore, as usual. Peter Bauland has summarized this disposition: "One of the main features of Dürrenmatt's effectiveness is that he deals with ethical problems with both wit and humor." [3] For example, Schwitter, the protagonist, cannot believe in his own demonstrable and numerous resurrections from death, while those around him can and do. Accepting the fact of God's providence, the believers die, actually at an alarming rate; but Schwitter, despite the vigorous pursuit of the science of dying (he carries funeral candles with him), remains

---

[1] Produced in Zürich on January 20, 1966.

[2] Heinz Beckmann in his review of the première performance of the play (in *der rheinische Merkur*) condemns especially its cynicism: "We are cynical, indeed, in order to put up with life, to protect ourselves against injuries, because we are so thin-skinned [*verwundbar*] while we go on living. But when life is over with, in the 'hour of truth?' [What then?] Yes, when truth becomes a Frau Nomsen [a washroom attendant], then naturally one becomes cynical or bourgeois or both at the same time."

[3] Bauland, p. 198.

unexplainably alive. Actually, Schwitter's name suggests *Zwitter-wesen,* a being between two worlds, and perhaps also *Schweizer,* "Swiss." Dürrenmatt's wit again comes into play with his depiction of the Lazarus-like Schwitter as an implacable realist and agnostic. "Dying is nothing tragic," he insists, as he makes his entrance. His *Weltanschauung* is strictly scientific and rationalistic, as described by his friend and critic Friedrich Georgen in a premature eulogy: "There was for him nothing but sheer reality [*die nackte Realität*]." [4]

Manifestation of Schwitter's conviction that life is sufficient unto itself, that one world is enough, constitutes the action in a play whose appeal is cerebral rather than visual. Thus Schwitter makes use of his dying as the prime element in his seduction of Auguste, an artist's model married to the man now occupying the garret where Schwitter began his career and where he hopes to end it. Coincidentally there are similarities between Dürrenmatt and Schwitter: both began their careers in the graphic arts; one of Schwitter's stories as described in the play is pronouncedly like *Der Besuch der alten Dame.* In *Der Meteor* Schwitter responds to each further intrusion on his setting the scene for his imminent death with statements indicating his lack of belief in a world transcending the real one. On this point Friedrich Georgen is also specific, noting: "He lacked [all] faith." [5] One of the first to intrude on Schwitter's dying is Pastor Lutz, whose faith in God has only been confirmed by the miracle which God has ordained in the life of Schwitter. The minister, wearied by the effort to secure a place for belief in an unbelieving world, assures Schwitter: "God chose you, Mr. Schwitter, so that the blind might see and so that the godless might believe in Him." [6] Now it becomes apparent that the man who has accepted God as his maker and redeemer has understood life and rightly lived it and can therefore leave it: Lutz dies. Schwitter goes on, trying to maintain his independence from the supernatural. "Dying is unhuman [*unmenschlich*]," he exclaims. [7]

Elucidation of Schwitter's inhumane treatment of his fourth wife Olga, his debasement of her into an object and of love into sex, follows in a series of encounters between the always dying, but never

---

[4] Friedrich Dürrenmatt, *Der Meteor* (Zürich, 1967), pp. 10, 41.

[5] Ibid., p. 41.

[6] Ibid., p. 18. One thinks naturally of Dürrenmatt's early play *Der Blinde.*

[7] *Der Meteor,* p. 36.

dead great man and his visitors, who try to shake him in his conviction that "life is horrible, blind and transitory," a matter of chance. [8]
Olga, a former prostitute, believing that her husband has ruined her
by depreciating her love for him, commits suicide; once more in
the throes of an inconclusive death, Schwitter is informed of her
successful dying. Again to establish his lack of conscience, he causes
the destruction of another — a total stranger, Muheim — whom
he turns into a murderer. Somewhat like da Ponte in *Der Blinde,* he
wishes to establish that "there are only men and that everything
that happens comes from man, good and bad fortune [alike]." [9]

Others suffer, too, from Schwitter's stubborn adherence to a code
of morality based upon the things of this world. Love of money
keeps him from expressing love for his son; the code specifies that,
since Jochen, the son, does not deserve his father's money, he must
not have it; he is deprived of his just inheritance. In a final cynical
act Schwitter converts all his wealth into cash and burns it.

Schwitter's detrimental effect on all those drawn, like flies into
the spider's web, to his garret [10] reaches a climax in his confrontation with his mother-in-law, Frau Nomsen (perhaps the name is
intended to suggest "nonsense"). In this rest-room attendant the
talented man finds his equal. "I was somewhat your equal morally
and in business matters," he tells her. [11] He has at last acquired
insight into the falsity of his position, the blasphemy of his belief
in nothing but mathematical chance. The title of the play represents
a concept behind which lurks the disillusionment inherent in a belief
in wisdom alone—the product of man's rationality: for a scientist
the meteor is, far from being a sign from heaven, only matter falling
through space, flaming as it expires. Schwitter wants to tell Frau
Nomsen something about a wisdom acquired intuitively, a wisdom
that is not based on the selling of one's children into prostitution
because only thus can they be saved from the wickedness of the
world; he describes for her his own defence against the world, his
amorality. "Guilt, redemption, justice, freedom, mercy, love, I dis-
pense with these noble excuses and rationalizations, which mankind

---

[8] Ibid., p. 68.

[9] *Komödien II,* p. 147.

[10] Included is his physician, Dr. Schlatter. Incidentally, Bonhoeffer men-
tions a Dr. Schlatter who was a teacher of ethics.

[11] *Der Meteor,* p. 68.

needs for its arrangements and plundering [*Raubzüge*]." His new-found perspicacity reaches the pinnacle of insight into himself: "I surrounded myself with invented people because I couldn't find my way through to real ones, for reality is not the same as literature [*am Schreibtisch faßbar*].... My life was not worth my living it." [12]

The last-minute, only-hinted-at conversion of Schwitter, his descent from a self-made tower of Babel, a rationalistic structure of morality, resembles that of Möbius in *Die Physiker*; Dürrenmatt did in fact begin writing *Der Meteor* at the time when he was occupied with *Die Physiker*. The technique in the two plays is strikingly similar: adherence to the three unities, a simple plot, a denouement explicitly tragic (Schwitter never dies), containing, however, an implicit resolution of the problem. As Fräulein Doktor von Zahnd cancels out the reckoning of Möbius, so Frau Nomsen confronts Schwitter with the futility of his *Weltanschauung*, which is the source of his frustration nad his inability to die. "Death is the only reality," he confesses finally to the woman, who is already beyond his reach. [13] His realization of this factor essential to an understanding of life coincides with Bonhoeffer's thinking: "We are paying more attention to dying than to death. We are more concerned to get over the act of dying than to overcome death.... There is a real difference between the two things; the one is within the scope of human possibilities, the other means resurrection. It is ... from the resurrection of Christ that a new and purifying wind can blow through our present world." [14] This conviction seems to underlie Dürrenmatt's playing with the themes of death and resurrection embodied in *Der Meteor*.

Bonhoeffer's morality parallels Dürrenmatt's morality in the ten major plays. In *Letters and Papers from Prison* Bonhoeffer sums up the moral history of mankind in modern times, as Dürrenmatt does in his plays: "We thought we could make our way in life with reason and justice, and when both failed, we felt that we were at the end of our tether." "We have spent too much time in thinking, supposing that if we weigh in advance the possibilities of any action, it will happen automatically. We have learnt, rather too late, that

---

[12] Ibid.
[13] Ibid.
[14] Bonhoeffer, p. 132.

action comes, not from thought, but from a readiness for responsibility.... 'Not every one who says to me, "Lord, Lord," shall enter the kingdom of heaven, but he who *does* the will of my Father who is in heaven,' said Jesus." [15]

In the realm of literature Dürrenmatt's plays make a similar statement about the kinds of morality and urge the acceptance of that kind which sees in a loving relationship between men and between men and God the only basis for a moral life. Dürrenmatt's approach (like Schwitter's) to this philosophy was at first hesitant. The early plays are the plays of a doubter. The first step toward commitment to a belief in love as the key to ethical behavior was made in *Die Ehe des Herrn Mississippi*. Thereafter, each of the plays (except *Frank der Fünfte*) contains a confrontation with the new morality. Akki, Ill, Augias and, less prominently, Möbius and Schwitter represent Dürrenmatt's allegiance to the single standard of love. Although he has properly pointed out that his plays are not philosophic or religious tracts (rather they are theatrical treats), they are, because of their probing of the dilemmas of faith in the modern world and their espousal of a solution, the new morality —relevant and of lasting value.

---

[15] Ibid., pp. 159, 158.

SELECTED BIBLIOGRAPHY

ALLEMANN, BEDA. "Dürrenmatt: *Es steht geschrieben*." In *Das deutsche Drama*, edited by Benno von Wiese, vol. 2. Düsseldorf, 1958.

BÄNZIGER, HANS. *Frisch und Dürrenmatt*. Bern, 1960.

BAULAND, PETER. *The Hooded Eagle*. Syracuse, N. Y., 1968.

BONHOEFFER, DIETRICH. *Letters and Papers from Prison*, translator anonymous. Rev. ed. New York, 1967.

BROCK-SULZER, ELISABETH. *Friedrich Dürrenmatt*. Zürich, 1964.

DAVIAU, DONALD G. "Justice in the Works of Friedrich Dürrenmatt." *Kentucky Foreign Language Quarterly* 9 (1962).

DÜRRENMATT, FRIEDRICH. *Der Besuch der alten Dame*. Edited by Paul Kurt Ackermann. Boston, 1957.

————. "Interview." *Journal of Modern Literature* 1 (1970).

————. *Komödien I*. Zürich, 1957.

————. *Komödien II und frühe Stücke*. Zürich, 1963.

————. *Der Meteor*, Zürich, 1967.

————. *Die Physiker*. Edited by Robert E. Helbling. New York, 1965.

————. "Rede an die Kritiker." In *Bestand und Versuch*. Zürich, 1964.

————. *Theaterprobleme*. Zürich, 1963.

FLETCHER, JOSEPH. *Moral Responsibility*. Philadelphia, 1967.

GASSNER, JOHN. *Theatre at the Crossroads*. New York, 1960.

GEIßLER, ROLF, ed. "Friedrich Dürrenmatt." *In Zur Interpretation des modernen Dramas*. Frankfurt am Main, n. d.

GUTHKE, KARL. *Geschichte und Poetik der deutschen Tragikomödie*. Göttingen, 1961.

JÄGGI, WILLY; BENN, GOTTFRIED; BROCK-SULZER, ELISABETH; BURI, FRITZ; GRIMM, REINHOLD; MEYER, HANS; and OBERLE, WERNER. *Der unbequeme Dürrenmatt*. Basel, 1962.

JAUSLIN, CHRISTIAN MARKUS. *Friedrich Dürrenmatt*. Zürich, 1964.

JENS, WALTER. *Statt einer Literaturgeschichte*. Tübingen, n. d.

LOHNER, EDGAR, and HANNUM, HUNTER G., eds. *Modern German Drama*. Boston, 1966.

NIEBUHR, REINHOLD. *An Interpretation of Christian Ethics*. New York, 1956.

OTTEN, ANNA, ed. *Mensch und Zeit*. New York, 1966.

REGENSTEINER, HENRY, ed. *Drei Hörspiele von Friedrich Dürrenmatt*. New York, 1965.

ROBINSON, JOHN A. T. *Honest to God*. Philadelphia, 1963.

STRELKA, JOSEF. *Brecht, Horvath, Dürrenmatt*. Vienna, 1962.

INDEX